JESUS

Dictations received by the Messenger
Tatyana Nicholaevna Mickushina
from 2005 through 2013

UDC 141.339=111=03.161.1
BBC 87.7+86.4

M59 Mickushina, T.N.

JESUS.

Masters of Wisdom / T.N. Mickushina.
– 2017. – 148 pages – ("Masters of Wisdom" series).

This book is a part of the Masters of Wisdom series.

This series of books presents a collection of Messages from different Masters who are most well-known to modern humanity. These Messages were transmitted through the Messenger Tatyana N. Mickushina, who has been working under the guidance of the Masters of Wisdom since 2004. Using a special method, T. N. Mickushina has received Messages from over 50 Beings of Light.

The book contains the Messages of Beloved Jesus. They give an in-depth the Teaching of Love for all Life, including to its enemies , the Teaching of Healing, the Teaching of the Inner Path, which lies in our hearts. Beloved Jesus gives knowledge of the Laws of Karma and Reincarnation, lost in modern Christianity, about the Kingdom of Heaven as a state of our consciousness.

UDC 141.339
BBC 87.7+86.4

Artwork for cover by Munir Alawi
www.muniralawi.info

ISBN-13: 978-1973908401
ISBN-10: 1973908409

Contents

I wish to help each one of you

**On the foundations of the Teaching and
the continuity of the transmission of the Teaching**

Jesus Christ
A Great Master. The founder of Christianity.

Jesus Christ is the Great Teacher who brought the people of the world the message of the Kingdom of God and the way in which to enter it. Jesus gave the world the commandment of Love: love for the Lord and love for one's neighbor.

In fact, Jesus is the creator of the Teaching of Life, which can be defined as the ethics of Love. It is the ethics of Love that formed the basis of Christianity.

Time and place of birth. Family. Early childhood.

The parents of Jesus, Mary and Joseph the carpenter, lived in Galilee, a small village of Nazareth. They both came from the family of David. Due to the population census that took place at that time, they went to Judaea, where their family had originated. Here, in Judaea, in Bethlehem, which is south of Jerusalem, Jesus was born[1].

---

[1] Jesus is the Greek form of the Jewish name Jeshua or Yeshua.

The date of birth seems to be obvious, since a new age began from the birth of Christ. However, that date was suggested by monk Dionysius 600 years later. It was accepted despite the obvious discrepancy that king Herod was still alive at the time when Christ was born.

New testaments do not provide Jesus's date of birth. The Gospel of Matthew describes the unusual circumstances that accompanied the birth of the Great Spirit. "After Jesus was born in Bethlehem in Judea, during the time of King Herod, Magi[2] from the East came to Jerusalem and asked, 'Where is the one who has been born king of the Jews? We saw His star when it rose and have come to worship Him' " (*New International Version*, Matthew 2:1-7). The Magi brought baby Jesus valuable gifts — gold, frankincense and myrrh — which in ancient times were usually gifted to kings and other

---

[2] In the modern Bible versions only one meaning of the Magi is given – the meaning of wise men. In the original version, the word "magicians" was used.

important people as a token of special reverence.

For a long time, the magicians had predicted that when planets Saturn and Jupiter come into a special conjunction, an Avatar (a Divine Incarnation) should be born. The Star that led the Magi occurred during that conjunction of planets. It appeared in Pisces which is known to astrologists to govern Judaea. That is why the Magi departed to Judaea, and their journey lasted for about one year.

In 1604, a prominent German astronomer, Johannes Kepler, was the first person to calculate the date of the conjunction of these planets — 7 B.C. In 1925, Chaldean astrological tables about the conjunction of planets Saturn and Jupiter in Pisces were deciphered. That conjunction had been carefully observed by Babylonian astronomers during a period of six months. The scientists determined the date of their observations to be 7 B.C. The Bible Encyclopedia (chapter "Herod") states that Jesus was born in the "thirty third year of Herod's reign," which is 7 B.C.

Jesus's Parents. Early years.

Jesus called His father the best of the fathers. He was a great soul[3], the keeper of Jesus and Mary.

---

[3] One of Saint Germain's incarnations.

Jesus's first teacher was His mother, whose pure heart and devotion to Divinity allowed for the Holy Spirit to be embodied. He learned from His mother that "the Word of God is saved by His prophets." During Sukkot, a seven-lamp menorah was lit in His parents' house and sacred stories were read. According to the legends, Jesus showed an interest in learning Jewish sacred scriptures from the age of five. Later, He exceeded His classmates in studying. He often caused dissatisfaction in His teachers, who blindly followed the words in the text while Jesus was striving to comprehend the meaning and spirit of the scriptures.

Nazareth, where Jesus's family lived, was located along the route of many caravans. Travelers who had been to many countries, especially those who had knowledge, attracted the child. He spoke with them, absorbed their teachings and often surprised them with His deep perception of sacred knowledge. Some of them stayed in Nazareth longer in order expand the mystic knowledge of this unusual child.

At the age of thirteen, during Passover, young Jesus got "in the center of the most prominent scientists and teachers of the Law of Israel…it was unheard of for an adolescent to speak freely in the presence of old masters, and it was wondrous that He took the liberty of objecting, speculating, and teaching in such an environment!" "The legends say that after Jesus's talk at the temple and after His parents found Him, the members of a secret organization of magicians addressed the parents. The parents finally agreed and the wise men took Jesus to their residence in order to give Him education that would be suitable for the aspirations of His soul and His mind." (Yogi Ramacharaka. "The Life of Jesus Christ.")

According to another legend, soon after that talk with the wise men at the temple, the parents sent their son to a deserted area of southern Judea (near the shores of the Dead Sea) to study in the community of the Essenes. At the age of 19, Jesus was accepted into an Essene monastery which was the concentration of the mystical science; it had a wonderful library of occult books, and hosted travelers from Iran and India on their way to Egypt. After learning the secret doctrine of the Essenes, Jesus left for Egypt. "For Egypt was one of the world centers, where true mysteries were kept….that is where young Jesus received the highest Initiation that prepared Him for the Royal priesthood." (Annie Besant.)

There are stories in the legends of Iran, India, and Tibet about a young master, Issa, who had once visited them and who studied their teachings and secret knowledge. The Brahmans and Buddhists have stories about the sermons of the young master directed against

10

caste limitations that had caused rebellions of priests against Him. For them, He was a dangerous rebel. Jesus-Issa always objected to the mischief-making and hypocrisy of the clergy, and He strived to return the people to the genuine spirit.

L. Dmitrieva, referencing the book "The Brotherhood of Graal" by Richard Rudzitis, says that "Christ (The Great Pilgrim) was in the Himalayas, in Shamballa, in the Great White Brotherhood, and spent three years there (L. Dmitrieva, *The Secret Doctrine of H. Blavatsky*, Part 3). In the same book she writes "the Tibetan Bible retells the life of saint 'Issa — the best of human sons.' This manuscript (the Tibetan Bible) was found in one of the Tibetan monasteries by the Russian scholar N. Notovich."

It is said that Jesus returned to Judea and began His Great Service after thirty years of travel, when He was already of a mature age.

The Great Service

Jesus began His Great Service — teaching the truth to the people of Israel — with baptism received from John. Why is this so? Perhaps, the answer lies in the legend that says that after His return to the Motherland, Jesus lived with the Essenes for about a year. The Essenes lived in a closed community near the Dead Sea. That is where He learned about the priesthood of John and made an intention to go to the place where he served, which was close to the Dead Sea, at the shore of the Jordan River. The Essene wise men notified John that a great Master would come to him, and that he should prepare the people for His appearance. Many people asked John about whether he was the Christ, and John would say that he was only preparing the path for the Lord. "I baptize you with water for repentance. But after me comes one who is more powerful than I, whose sandals I am not worthy to carry. He will baptize you with the Holy Spirit and fire." (Matthew 3:11). Thus, Jesus's task was clearly outlined: to open the eyes of the people to the spiritual, Divine plan; to carry the fire of love and wisdom to the people. For three years the Master and His disciples were constantly travelling, often crossing Palestine from south to north and back. From the place of baptism in the Jordan River, He went north, to Galilea, and from there He went south, all the way across the country to Jerusalem, to celebrate the first Holy Passover after His return from His journey. Jesus went to the temple along with His disciples. He saw how relentlessly the lambs were killed for sacrifice right inside the temple, demonstrating all the hypocrisy of the heartless ceremony. He saw herds of

cattle and sheep, bargainers and merchants right in the temple. After seeing this blasphemy, "He made a whip out of cords, and drove all from the temple courts, both sheep and cattle. To those who sold doves He said, 'Get these out of here! Stop turning my Father's house into a market!' " (John 2:15-16). The clergy could not forgive Jesus for His forcible assertion of righteousness.

The following months were again spent travelling across Judaea, Samaria, and Galilea. Everywhere He went, Jesus founded groups of disciples, mostly from the poor and disadvantaged. When He found out about the death of John the Baptist, Jesus went to the desert to think about the work that was ahead of Him: John's work was awaiting Him. While before He was a quiet teacher of the few, now He spoke in front of crowds of people as a "passionate preacher and speaker...and many educated people came to listen to...His calls to truthfulness, virtuous living and contemplation." (Yogi Ramacharaka. "The Life of Jesus Christ.")

According to legend, when Jesus was visiting Nazareth, He went to a local synagogue. Due to His birth and education, He could lead a Jewish service and give sermons as a rabbi, or a clergy member. He began His sermon from the text of the prophet Isaiah: "The Spirit of the Lord GOD is upon me, because the LORD has anointed me to proclaim good news to the poor. He has sent me to bind up the brokenhearted." (Isaiah 61:1). "Today the Holy Scripture is becoming reality in front of you," Jesus proclaimed to the amazed Nazareans, and He began to say that He had come to bear the Truth; He called to the achievements of the spirit, exposed the formalism of the clergy and condemned the mercantile ceremonies. The enraged crowd dragged Jesus across the city streets. He did not resist. Only when they brought Him close to a cliff drop, He peacefully went through the crowd, as His time had not come yet. That is when Jesus said His famous phrase: "A prophet is not without honor, except in his hometown and among his relatives and in his own household." Jesus had to leave His hometown, Nazareth, together with His mother and disciples and get settled in Capernaum.

In Capernaum, Jesus began to turn the group of His disciples into a labor organization and gradually teach them the knowledge that He had Himself. "There was a lot of astonishment among the disciples when He wanted to work together with them, in order to earn the food... Several of the most jealous disciples turned away exactly because of such constant labor" (*Supermundane*, Part I, 155, Russian version). This is when the stream of His amazing wonders and

healings began. He healed the son of a courtier from a distance, He healed with a touch, or the powerful words "heal" or "rise and go." He healed the blind and the disabled, those with paralysis or leprosy, those who were possessed or mentally ill. He brought the dead back to life, filled fishermen's nets with fish; and He created fish and bread to feed thousands of hungry people who had come to listen to Him. He walked on the water and pacified the hurricane. He used all of His occult knowledge about the mysteries of nature and the human spirit for the people. He did not take for Himself; He gave generously, in spite of the distrust of the crowds, intolerance of the Pharisees, opposition of the doctors and the clergy. So went the Great Pilgrim across the country. "Jesus went throughout all the towns and villages, teaching in their synagogues, proclaiming the good news (the Gospels/New Testament) of the kingdom and healing every disease and sickness." (Matthew 9:35).

The following section is taken from the book *Supermundane*, Part I, 151-152:

"…every Great Teacher is associated with healing and the arts." The Great Pilgrim[4] was especially prominent in these qualities. "There was much healing, mainly of two kinds, when people came to Him, or when He Himself would touch a person because He saw the onset of an illness. Often the ailing one did not understand why the Stranger had touched him. Such an act represented true generosity on the part of the Great Spirit, who, like a tireless gardener, sowed such seeds of goodness."

"His words about Beauty also do not appear often in the Apocrypha, but they were said nonetheless. The Teacher drew people's attention to beautiful flowers and

---

[4] Christ was called by this name in the book "*Supermundane*, The Inner Life," Book 1, 1938. Published by Agni Yoga Society)

to the radiance of the sun. He also encouraged group singing, for it is the most powerful method of achieving harmonious vibrations. The Teacher did not insist on this specific aspect of music and singing, but simply advocated joy and inspiration."

"There were those among the disciples and followers whose lives were filled with misery and daily hardship. The Teacher would first help them by uplifting their spirits, and only when balance was established would He discuss their problems. He never condemned their past, but led them into the future. The Teacher could clearly see the future, but only revealed it according to the consciousness of His disciples. Nor did He hesitate to use severe words to revive the dead consciousness."

"Thus the Healer and Creator proceeded on His Way."

"He did not avoid mingling with people. He visited their festivals and discussed their daily needs, but few noticed the wise advice that was given with a smile and words of encouragement. His smile was beautiful. His intimate tenderness was not always appreciated by the disciples, who sometimes even criticized Him, believing that He should not have given so much attention to people of no importance. However, wonderful souls were revealed and made manifest by His smiles. He was criticized for talking to women, yet it was women who preserved the Teaching. He was also criticized for association with so-called heathens by those who forgot that the Teacher came to all people, not just to one sect. It was part of His lofty achievements to accept insults with equanimity."

"We mention these condemnations because through them the Image of the Great Pilgrim is shown to be more human. If He had not come into contact with life and had not suffered, His deeds would not have been as great. No one realized how tormented He was by the many disturbed auras He came into contact

with in this way, but the thought of great achievement never left Him. The condemnation that He heard also contributed to the bearing of the achievement. "Thus the Great Teacher followed His ardent Path."

During the days of the third Passover, Jesus solemnly entered Jerusalem together with His disciples, greeted by the people, while the Sanhedrin[5] was already preparing a reprisal for Him. Based

------

[5] The Council was the supreme court of the highest priests of Judah, which consisted of 72 members, primarily of the Pharisee or Sadducee sects, with pontiff being the chair.

on Judas's accusation, Jesus was arrested and brought in front of the Council. The hearing, held at night, with members absent and court rules violated, found Jesus to be a dangerous rebel. Demanding a death penalty, the priests brought Jesus to Pilate[6], and then to Herod Antipas[7], and back to Pilate. Not seeing Jesus's guilt, Pilate was trying to change the death penalty to a ruthless flagellation and release the prisoner in honor of the holiday, but the priests and the people whom they provoked demanded crucifixion. Jesus was crucified next to two villains.

Jesus's Prayer

Christ gave His disciples only one prayer. "In this prayer, He enclosed an ancient teaching that had existed long before Him and that He had received by tradition… all the Teaching that He had learned, He wished to enclose in the prayer 'Our Father,' hoping that people would plant that seed in their soul…would cultivate it, in order to grow a wonderful tree of the Initiation Science which He had left us." (Omraam Mikhaël Aïvanhov, "The True Meaning of Christ's Teaching.") "Our Father, who art in heaven, hallowed be thy Name, thy kingdom come, thy will be done, on earth as it is in heaven. Give us this day our daily bread; and forgive us our trespasses, as we forgive those who trespass

---

[6] Pontius Pilate – the Roman governor, or the Procurator of Judea.

[7] Herod Antipas – one of the Roman deputies, he had a formal title of the King.

against us, and lead us not into temptation, but deliver us from evil. For thine is the kingdom, and the power, and the glory, forever. Amen." (Matthew 6:9-13).

Christ's Sacred Teaching

"The Great Pilgrim advocated the broadening of consciousness, and repeatedly taught, 'Open your eyes and ears.' Certainly, He did not invite people to open their eyes and ears only to His particular Teachings, but meant that only the expansion of consciousness leads to profound realization. But, alas, one cannot thread a needle with a rope, and a great message cannot penetrate a small ear. One can imagine how much of His Teaching never reached the consciousness of His listeners." (*Supermundane*, Part I, 176).

All ancient Eastern religions had two teachings: one was the secret, sacred teaching for the disciples of Mysteries, and the other teaching was for the "outsiders" those whose consciousness was not ready to take in the sacred knowledge. There are many references, including those in the Gospel, of the Mystery Teachings of Jesus, or Mystery Teachings of the Kingdom. Christ clearly talks about it to His disciples: "The secret of the kingdom of God has been given to you. But to those on the outside everything is said in parables." (Mark 4:11). In ancient scriptures, the Initiated ones were referred to as the Advanced and the Wise. The so-called first initiation was from the water and the Spirit. Jesus says to Pharisee Nicodemus: "Very truly I tell you, no one can enter the

kingdom of God unless they are born of water and the Spirit. Flesh gives birth to flesh, but the Spirit gives birth to spirit." (John 3:5-6). The next initiation was from the Holy Spirit and the Fire. John the Baptist was preaching: "I baptize you with water for repentance, but He who is coming after me <...> will baptize you with the Holy Spirit and fire" (Matthew 3:11).

"Enter through the narrow gate. For wide is the gate and broad is the road that leads to destruction, and many enter through it. But small is the gate and narrow the road that leads to life, and only a few find it." (Matthew 7:13, 14). This is the highest occult Teaching. "The narrow gate" was the gate of the Initiation, and through it the initiate came to the Holy Kingdom. However, only few can enter that gate, and only those whose efforts are directed at constant perfection, and whose life is directed at giving to people. One can consider this perspective when analyzing Jesus's words to His disciples "you are gods" (John 10:34) and His call: "You therefore must be perfect, as your heavenly Father is perfect" (Matthew 5:48).

Jesus taught His disciples to live and act in such a way so that people would notice their spiritual light and comprehend it: "You are the light of the world <...> let your light shine before others, so that they may see your good deeds and give glory to your Father in heaven" (Matthew 5:14, 16). "You are the salt of the earth" (Matthew 5:13). The function of the salt is to give flavor to the food; the duty of the Initiated is to give the taste of spirituality to mankind.

The disciples received the sacred knowledge directly from the Great Master, and that awakened in them their hidden natural powers. During the second year of instruction, He could send His chosen ones to preach and help the needy in health, giving them the directive: "You received without paying; give without pay," "be wise as serpents and innocent as doves" (Matthew 10:8, 16).

The Master knew that His death was nearing and was preparing His disciples for Service, sending them into different towns of the country. "He entrusted His disciples to take...magnets (the objects that were close to the Great Pilgrim) to far away countries. One must remember how far His heralds went. People did not know them, but they still felt the importance of such messengers and hated them, as people hate everything that is incomprehensible." (*Supermundane*, Book I, 155, Russian version).

22

"...the Great Pilgrim could direct people to the Highest just by His glance. The Teacher used to say, 'Friends, you find ample time for everything, but for the Highest you have only a few moments. If you had dedicated only the time you waste in the dining-hall to the Highest, you would have become teachers by now!' Thus, in practical terms, He taught the advantage of elevated thinking." (*Supermundane*, Book I, 156).

Christ affirmed the indefeasible Law of reincarnation with His words: "… a hundredfold now in this time, houses and brothers and sisters and mothers and children and lands, along with persecutions, and in the age to come eternal life. But many who are first will be last, and the last first." (Mark 10:30-31). Other words from the fourth Gospel also illustrate the law of reincarnation: "So the Jews said to him, 'You are not yet fifty years old, and you have seen Abraham?' Jesus said to them, 'Very truly, I say to you, before Abraham was born, I am!' " (John 8:57-58).

Knowing the Law of Karma, Jesus taught responsibility for one's deeds. "I tell you, on the day of judgment everyone will have to give account for every careless word they have spoken." (Matthew 12:36). "First be reconciled to your brother, and then come and offer your gift. Settle matters quickly with your accuser while you are going with him to court." (Matthew 5:24-25). "… whatever you bind on earth will be bound in heaven, and whatever you loose on earth will be loosed in heaven." (Matthew 16:19).

Being an Initiated one, the Master knew that the cosmic Law of Karma, or the Law of Retribution, gives back to people not only based on their deeds, but also based on their desires and thoughts; that is why even a lustful look at a woman must be punished. One cannot avoid the punishment. If there are no visible witnesses, there is an invisible witness — the Law of Karma. "There is nothing concealed that will not be disclosed, or hidden that will not be known." (Luke 12:2). Knowing the power of thought, Christ warned His contemporaries to act and think justly. "Knowing their thoughts, Jesus said, 'Why do you entertain evil thoughts in your hearts?' " (Matthew 9:4). "So in everything, do to others what you would have them do to you, for this sums up the Law and the Prophets." (Matthew 7:12).

"The Teacher also said, 'Beware of negative thoughts. They will turn against you and will burden you like an abominable leprosy. But good thoughts rise upward and will lift you with them. You must know the power of the healing light and deadly darkness that man carries within himself.' "

"He also said, 'You are used to fearing death because you were not taught about the passing into a better World.' "

"And He also said, 'You must realize that good friends will continue to work together there, just as here.' Thus the Great Pilgrim continued teaching about the eternal values and the power of thought, but His Teachings were comprehended by only a few." (*Supermundane*, Book I, 160)

Even in the Gospels that had been distorted in later additions, Christ's assertions of the Divine Feminine have

24

been preserved. In the fallen woman Mary Magdalene, He sees not a sinner but a heart that deeply feels Love for the Master, and later becomes a devoted disciple. Among the people who were the closest to Him, there were women that are also mentioned in the Gospels. One of His commandments, just as those of other

Great Wisemen, is to honor your father and your mother. "For God commanded, 'Honor your father and your mother,' and, 'Whoever reviles their father or mother must surely die.' " (Matthew 15:4).

The Great Master loved children and allowed them close to Him, as He saw in them the advancement of mankind: "Let the little children come to me and do not hinder them, for the kingdom of heaven belongs to such as these." (Matthew 19:13-14).

Christ's Mission

Christ's coming 2000 years ago denoted not only the beginning of a new era (the era of Pisces), but also the coming of the New World. The Great Master saw the distant future when predicting His Advent and the coming of the fire energies of the New World: the new

Sky and the new Earth, "then the old ones will no longer be remembered." Like Prometheus, Christ brought the Divine Fire of Love to the people: "I have come to bring fire on the earth, and how I wish it were already kindled!" (Luke 12:49).

Having predicted the coming of the Fire World, the Great Prophet showed how to prepare for Its Coming. His commandments of Love and spiritual perfection were left in the Gospels like precious pearls.

Christ's greatest Commandment is to love the Lord with all the heart and all the soul. The second commandment, like it, is to love your neighbor as yourself.

Love the Lord and love your neighbor.

Be perfect, as your heavenly Father is perfect.

Have unity.

Herald the Will of God.

Abide by the Divine Law.

Do not destroy the soul.

Do not lay up for yourselves treasures on earth, but lay up for yourselves treasures in heaven.

Show your deeds[8]

---

[8] "By their fruit you will recognize them. Do people pick grapes from thornbushes, or figs from thistles?" Mathew 7.16
"Thus, by their fruit you will recognize them." Mathew 7.20

Accept the child[9]

Judge not, that you be not judged.

Forgive others their trespasses.

Pray secretly.

Love your enemies.

Be joyful. Do not look gloomy.

"So in everything, do to others what you would have them do to you, for this sums up the Law and the Prophets." (Matthew 7:12)."If you would enter life, keep the commandments…You shall not murder, you shall not commit adultery, you shall not steal, you shall not give false testimony, honor your father and mother, and love your neighbor as yourself." (Matthew 19:17, 19).

The inner meaning of Christ's Teaching was that the earthly world is a temporary world, that is why we should prepare ourselves for the transition into the New World, the Divine World, which is the genuine home, from which human beings, the sons and daughters of God have come and where they will go back. "I am the good shepherd, and I know the Path home."

The path to God is an inner Path. To open up that Path was the Mission, the inner Teaching of

---

[9] "But Jesus said, Suffer little children, and forbid them not, to come unto me: for of such is the kingdom of heaven." Mathew 19.14

"…and said, "Amen, I say to you, unless you turn and become like children,* you will not enter the kingdom of heaven." Mathew 18.3

Christ. Christ had come to show the Path and become an example of how each of us can follow that Path. "Whoever believes in me will also do the works that I have been doing." (John 14:12). In order to enter the Divine world, one must get rid of the carnal, mortal being and put on the spiritual being. In other words, one must attain the level of Christ, Christ Consciousness, which is the intermediary between the lower consciousness of the carnal mind and the higher Divine Consciousness. This inner Teaching of Christ had been replaced by the false Teaching about the only Son of God, and the cult of worshiping Christ was created.

The only Path to God is to learn God's Laws and begin to create Perfection in the name of the common good and brotherhood on Earth.

One of Christ's tasks was to prove the immortal nature of the human spirit. He proved this powerfully by His resurrection in the subtle body after His physical death. "When talking about His resurrection, Christ did not have in mind His conscious passing into the Subtle World, but actually His appearance in a subtle body amidst physical conditions. Of course, such an appearance of the physically dead person in the materialized subtle body was striking proof of His resurrection and thus strengthened the disciples' faith in His Teaching." (Letters of Helena Roerich, Volume II). The rising from death inspired people and convinced them in the truthfulness of Christ's Teachings more than any other arguments. "The phenomenon of the materialization of the subtle body of the Teacher strengthened the belief of the disciples in the reality of the Invisible World. Not all of them were able to perceive the essence of that world, but the window had at least been opened to a certain degree." (*Supermundane*, Book I, 172).

Leaving the earthly plane, the Great Master voluntarily took on the great suffering, in order to embody with His sacrifice His Teachings of Love and Service to all people of Earth. The Son of Man had specifically come on Earth in order to serve the people. "Greater love has no one than this: to lay down one's life for one's friends." (John 15:13). Christ imprinted this Teaching of Love that He brought by His blood, and by the act of Great Sacrifice He imprinted the strength of Spirit over the physical matter of body and the immortality of the spirit.

Adapted from the book "The Great Moralists – the Founders of World Religions"[10]

Prepared by Elena Ilyina

---

[10] *"The Great Moralists – the Founders of World Religions" by Valentina Polyan (Omsk; Publishing House "Sirius," 2009, Russian version)*

The Kingdom of Heaven is the state of your consciousness. And when you reach a certain level of your consciousness evolution, you acquire access to this Kingdom of Heaven.

Jesus, March 21, 2005

I appeal to those of you who experience a special affinity for me

March 21, 2005

I AM Jesus. I have come through this Messenger of God.

About 2000 years have passed since my last incarnation on the earth. I am happy to use an opportunity to give you a short Teaching through this Messenger.

You know that at the time of my incarnation I worked wonders and many people came to see them. Many fewer people came to listen to my Teachings. And only my 12 closest disciples were able to perceive that secret knowledge that I imparted.

This knowledge differed greatly from the religious beliefs of that time.

But I kept teaching because I was to sow the grains of the Truth in the hearts of at least a few of my followers.

What happened then? Those people who had fully adopted my Doctrine were prosecuted and executed.

Then other people emerged, opportunists, who managed to adapt my Doctrine to their mercenary interests and utilize this Doctrine for their own well-being, not taking care of the fact that they were misrepresenting the Divine Truth.

There is a great precipice between the Doctrine I brought into this world during my incarnation and the doctrine that is being given now in Christian churches, though the most advanced souls have understood this difference in the course of 2000 years. They have been guided by such understanding of my Teachings that emanated from their hearts but not from the dead letters of the distorted writings.

Each of these zealots of Spirit had a certain degree of inner contact with me.

And I have always answered the sincere aspirations of their hearts. I helped them as much as it was possible through the exhortations that they were receiving in Spirit.

And I continue my inner link with many incarnated individuals now.

I am saying this for those of you who feel a special affinity for me, maintained from life to life.

You do not need any external doctrine in order to feel the sweetness of our communion and my Love. External Doctrines just serve as a powerful spur to direct your consciousness. Regretfully, the existing official church does not give a big incentive to your aspiration to commune with me honestly.

Therefore, I appeal to those of you who feel a special affinity for me. I want you to know that I am open for contacts with you in your hearts.

I come to everybody who invites me, to everybody who has prepared his temple for receiving me.

Do not be frightened or despairing if our communion is not immediate. It is important for me that your vibrations should reach a certain level of purity. Then I will be able to dwell in you and to communicate with you.

Your aspiration to our communion will create a certain aspiration magnet, and I will have an opportunity to descend into your heart for our inner communion.

If you read attentively even that variant of the Gospels accessible for reading now, you will see that I have never called you to observe the external ceremonials. I have called you to follow the Path in your hearts.

And I have taught you to prepare your temple for the bridegroom's coming. Your bridegroom is your Christ Self.

When your lower bodies and your soul reach a certain grade of purity, you acquire an opportunity to commune with your Christ Self, you higher part. And through your Christ Self you acquire an opportunity to commune with all the Ascended Hosts.

In reality, for the process of our communication you do not need any outward messenger.

I give you my support, and peace, and consolation. You will find all this inside of your heart.

I will come to everybody who has missed me and is waiting for me. I promise to come to each of you and give you the very things that your hearts have been thirsting after for so long. I will give you knowledge about your Source, about the world you have come from and to where you aspire to return. I will help you to recollect your first love and give you knowledge about the Path that will lead you Home to your Father in Heaven.

Do not believe those who say that this kingdom is here or that kingdom is there. Do not believe those who talk you into building such a Kingdom in the external world regardless of the name they give it — the Kingdom of Heaven on Earth or communism.

You do not need to go to the world's end — to India, America, or Tibet — to seek this Kingdom.

The Kingdom of Heaven is the state of your consciousness. And when you reach a certain level of your consciousness evolution, you acquire access to this Kingdom of Heaven.

This is hard for you to understand, so I ask you to trust me.

Take my hand. Hold it firmly, and I will show you the way to this Kingdom, the entrance to which is inside of your heart.

Only first you have to give up freely those qualities that burden your hearts and prevent you from seeing me, even when I come to you and am standing right in front of your eyes.

You will not see me until you free yourselves from the load on your shoulders. This load is nothing else but your attachments to the world around you.

I will give you an exercise. Promise me to practice it every day.

Every day visualize a radiant dazzling Light straight in front of you. Feel a desire to join with this Light and to become one and indivisible with it. If this Light burns you and you cannot approach it, then there is something in you that does not let you find the state inherent in your true nature — the state of Light, Fire and Flame.

Think of what prevents you from doing this. What is not from Light in you? You do not need to try to get rid of all your imperfections immediately. Find only one trait in yourselves that, in your opinion, most of all prevents you from manifesting your true nature. If you do not know what this trait is, meditate on me, ask me, and I will tell you what this trait is. It will manifest itself in your life and you will wish to get rid of it.

You must have such a passionate desire to get rid of this bad habit or trait that you will be constantly asking me in your prayers to deliver you from it and help you overcome this imperfection of yours.

You can simply ask or you can pray. And the day will come when you will completely get rid of this habit or trait. Then start getting rid of your next imperfection.

Give all your imperfections to me. Ask me, and I will take them.

And there will be nothing in you that will prevent you from seeing me standing in front of you. I will only have to lead you by the hand into the Kingdom of Heaven, along the secret path hidden in a secret place inside your heart.

We will meet when that moment comes. I will come to you again and again until you are able to hear me and feel my Love.

**I AM Jesus,
your friend and brother on your Path.**

I took upon myself the sins of the world, but the main thing I did was to show you the Path

May 1, 2005

I AM Jesus Christ, having come to you today through this Messenger Tatyana.

I have come! Today is the day when the orthodox Christians celebrate the light holiday of Easter in memory of my resurrection after the crucifixion on the cross.

You know that both the symbol of crucifixion and the symbol of resurrection do not belong only to the event that took place on the earth 2000 years ago.

These are the symbols concerning each of you living on Earth now. Each of you must pass through your own crucifixion and resurrection. Therefore, let today's holiday serve as a reminder to you about your Path of initiations and the trials you are to overcome on this Path.

It does not mean, beloved, that you will necessarily be crucified as I was. And it does not mean, beloved, that you will be resurrected as I was. But these events will surely take place at the final stage of your initiations.

Your crucifixion will take place when you hang on the cross between life and death — between the life that is eternal and staying in your mortal world. You will realize the decay of the physical world around you and will feel a touch of the eternal world. And the feelings that you will experience during this initiation will be compared with the process of crucifixion that I happened to experience. Your physical body and all your higher bodies will suffer. You will feel not only your own pain but also the pain of every living creature suffering in your world. You will feel the imperfection of your world in its entirety.

You will encounter these imperfect states of consciousness around you. And you will make a choice and sacrifice yourself and everything you have, even your physical body, in order to help the suffering creatures around you who do not even know the reasons for their suffering.

Yes, beloved, those people who are ready for awakening and whose time has come experience such terrible pain and suffering now that they are ready to accept the help of everybody who will explain to them the reason for their pain.

And it will be good if there happens to be a person near them who has realized the state of being between the two worlds and made a choice in favor of the Divine world.

Beloved, many of you have gone through your crucifixion already and many are close to going through it. This is a state of your consciousness when you realize your destiny and when you sacrifice all your being for the good of all the living creatures. However, these living creatures, instead of thanking and lauding you, will try to humiliate and hurt you; they will persecute you and try to punish you.

And at the moment when it seems that you have no more strength to endure this superhuman exertion of all your forces, you will realize that these people do not know what they are doing. And you will forgive them all, and moreover, you will wish to take upon yourselves their sins that dim their eyes and prevent them from seeing the Truth.

It is then that you will go through your crucifixion on the cross of matter.

And after this you will be ready for your resurrection — the state of your full harmony with the Will of God and full liberation from human thoughts and feelings.

It is truly a resurrection because your Spirit will receive an opportunity to act through you. And you will become invulnerable to all the arrows aimed at you. Now there is nothing in your physical world that can do any harm to you.

You revive your spiritual energies and hold these energies in your physical plane. Nothing from the abomination of desolation around you can affect you any longer. On the contrary, beloved, and merely with your presence you can stop any manifestations of imperfection in your world.

You receive an additional opportunity to provide your possible service and help to the people around you because this help is now the help of the Heavens themselves. It is because there is already nothing in you that can distinguish your consciousness from the Divine one.

Do not believe those who will tell you that there was only one Son of God and only He alone could take upon himself all the sins of the world.

Yes, I took upon myself the sins of the world, but the main thing I did was show you the Path that you should follow and are following now already.

I gave you the Path, the Rose Path, covered with roses and thorns. And there is no other path to follow through which you may reach the Kingdom of your Father in Heaven.

Beloved, I am overwhelmed with the feeling of Love towards you. I see your service and I see how hard your life is at this time. Events develop so quickly that your consciousness can hardly find time to adapt to the fast change of the scenery.

Those who have stepped on the Path of service and follow it with confidence will receive the confirmation of the faultlessness of the chosen Path. You will receive this confirmation in the form of moments of soft joy and indescribable bliss descending upon you. Beloved, remember these moments; absorb these states of bliss with all the cells and atoms of your being. Catch these moments of bliss. They will give you strength and energy, and an opportunity to pass all your tests and trials on the Path.

Let Love be your constant companion during all the minutes of your life. If you do not experience the feeling of Love, then ask me, appeal to me, and I will do my best to return your Love to you.

Love is a sign on your Path, showing you that your Path is right.

You should not associate this feeling with any certain person, and you must not demand the reciprocation of Love in exchange. Though sometimes it is your Love towards a certain person that saves you during the most difficult periods of your trials.

When you love, you do not need anything more. You are ready just to experience this state and enjoy it. All your problems, all your imperfections and the imperfections of the world around you are dissolved by this unique solvent, primordially inherent in this universe.

The flame of the true Divine Love is able to make its home only in the hearts of those people who have not lost their link with the Divine world. It is the very feeling that is capable of raising your vibrations and bringing them into harmony with the constantly rising vibrations of your physical plane.

Those people who are not able to assimilate the energies of Love will feel more and more cut off from your world. Sooner or later they will decide either to resign themselves to the energy of Love or to leave this world forever, as they will not be able to stay in it any longer due to the big divergence in vibrations.

Beloved, I have been glad to use this opportunity to meet you today, as I know that on this day most of the people reading these lines celebrate the event of my resurrection. Let me join your commemoration and celebrate the triumph of resurrections of those of you who reached in your consciousness the state of resurrection of the Divine vibrations and who are fully in keeping with me and the other Ascended Masters.

This is a great victory, beloved, because you have reached the state enabling us to dwell in your temples!

You will not believe me if I say that there is a much smaller part of me in Heaven than the part that is dwelling now on Earth in your temples — in the temples of those who invited me to enter them and whose vibrations let me do it.

I will also tell you confidentially that the majority of the Ascended Masters who have kept their links with non-ascended mankind are also staying among you, in your bodies and in the bodies of your brothers and sisters.

The worlds are approaching each other. The time has come when our worlds are getting closer and closer to each other by their vibrations. And more and more of you, beloved, will come in touch with us and realize it with your external consciousness.

I have been delighted with our meeting today. I impart all the Love of my heart to you and accept the Love of your hearts.

I AM Jesus, your brother.

The Path of initiations that I teach is the Path of full humility before the Will of God, complete dedication and sacrifice

May 22, 2005

I AM Jesus, your elder brother and preceptor, having come to you through this Messenger.

I have come to reopen an eternal talk that will be vital for you until you dress up in the wedding garments and ascend into the Light.

Until that time you will be constantly busy separating in your consciousness the eternal things belonging to the Higher world from the things liable to decay belonging to the transient world.

Your reality shrouds you in a fog of illusion and distracts you from the work that is really your vocation. However, no matter how long you meander in the illusory world, an end will come to your wandering sooner or later. Many dedicated seekers of the Truth are mistaken and deluded when they suppose that the Path Home must represent a state of eternal bliss and love. It is right, but right as much as something can be right and true in your world.

The states of bliss, joy, love, and conciliation are the signs that you are on the right Path and that you have chosen the correct direction. But you will not be able to maintain a constantly even state of spirit in your world. My aim today is to give you an exhortation and to warn you about the possible inferior states of consciousness that you may encounter on your Path. But these states will not necessarily serve as evidence that you have gone astray.

A constant analysis and a constant identification of your states are exactly the things required of you on the entire length of your Path.

Imagine that you really started your Path at a time when the sun was shining, it was calm and everything was fragrant and blooming. You may consider it to be a right sign on the Path. But all of a sudden the wind and thunderclouds spring up and the thunder booms. All this does not necessarily indicate that you have gone astray. You are still moving in the right direction, in spite of the fact that the external circumstances have changed and your mood has darkened along with the change in the weather.

In exactly the same way you can feel the most elevated states of consciousness in your life. You may be at the peak of bliss. But suddenly your state may deteriorate without just cause. For no reason you feel causeless melancholy, depression, pointlessness of your existence and disbelief.

45

These states are not always the signs of your having gone astray, beloved. They simply show you that the time is ripe for you to pass the tests and trials on the Path. You have heard of the school of mysteries of Lord Maitreya. You have heard of the schools of initiations that have existed at all times.

If the path to God represented just a state of constant bliss and grace, why would these schools of initiations be necessary?

And why are the initiations necessary at all?

There are two persons inside of you. One is mortal and the other is immortal. These two persons have become so entangled during many million years of their existence on planet Earth that it will require considerable efforts to separate these two from one another. One of them is to stay on Earth and to return into Earth from where he has been taken. The other is to continue existence in another higher plane of reality.

When you start the process of separating these two persons from one another in your consciousness, it is sometimes quite difficult to perform such a separation. You literally have to cut to the quick. You have got used to identifying yourself with the individual whom you see in the mirror. But in fact, all the stages of initiations that you pass are aimed exactly at helping you to stop your self-identification with the reflection in the mirror. That's why they say that if you want to see your enemy, come up to the mirror and look into it.

In reality, all that you have considered to be your individuality during many lives is not you actually but represents that part of you that you must give up and with which you must stop identifying yourself.

That part of you that resists the process of knowing your new individuality will rise from the depth of your being, from your unconscious and subconscious, and protest. In your external consciousness you may not fully understand the reason for your melancholy, your despair and your state of extreme depression and irreparability.

It is difficult to analyze which energies have been activated in your four lower bodies in accordance with the cosmic period that has approached now. But these energies represent the unreal part of you. And the purpose of any test, beloved, is to remind you that you are merely disciples on the Path and that you are just passing the next exam. No matter how real your state of mind seems to you, you should constantly remember that it is just a test.

The more in your external consciousness you resist parting with the energy activated within you, the longer drawn-out is your test.

The most advanced disciples always remember that God has a right to put them to the tests that can cause the most, as one would think, unendurable states of consciousness. And at the minute of the upmost tension of all their strengths, when it seems that the sun will never shine again, they come up to the altar and say in their hearts, "**Lord, I know that this state of my consciousness is not real. I know, Lord, that this is merely a test. I am ready, oh Lord, to endure all the trials that You send me. And I will try to do this. You** have a right to send me any trials, oh Lord. And I am grateful for all the trials that You send me because I know that You love me and care about me. I ask You, oh Lord, to help me endure this trial and pass through it to the end."

The purpose of all the trials is to test one single quality, and that is your ability to give up the unreal part of yourself, first of all in your consciousness.

Thanks to the infinite mercy of Heaven you have an opportunity to go through your tests and trials and to pass your exams without leaving your usual life. You continue living your usual life, but if at your inner levels you have expressed a wish to go through the initiations while staying in the usual life, such a chance will be given to you, irrespective of whether you are aware of your asking in your external state of consciousness or not. That is why I have come today to explain the reason for the causeless gloomy states and various psychological problems to those of you who experience such states.

Yes, beloved, you have made a choice to go through training at the school of initiations without leaving your usual life. You have chosen an accelerated Path. Your soul has expressed a wish to go through initiations in this life so as not to wait for the next embodiment and for suitable conditions of training at the school of mysteries somewhere in silence and far from the highways of the modern civilization.

This Path of initiations, the Rose Path, is the Path that all of you should follow. I do not know another path. The separation of your real part from your unreal part is always accompanied by very painful and unpleasant feelings. Both the duration and the heaviness of such states will be determined by the level of resistance of your unreal part. Everything will be determined by the potency of your ego, beloved.

You know that I managed to give up my unreal part during those 40 days when I was staying in the desert. However, you know that afterwards this was followed by my service, my transfiguration, crucifixion, and ascension.

You will pass through constant trials and tests as long as you are in the physical plane of planet Earth. And, even if you give up the unreal part of yourself, you will not be able just to give up the rest of mankind as a bad job and to be as snug as a bug in a rug somewhere in Heaven.

Do not hope, beloved, that your ascension will put an end to your evolution, your tension, your work, and your responsibility. Everything will be just beginning. And the higher your abilities, the larger the weight you will take upon yourself and the more vital service you will perform.

You should come to like the tension. You should come to like the service.

The highest manifestation of your Love will be the compassion towards the entire mankind and all the living creatures, and you will be ready to sacrifice for the sake of the salvation of mankind. You will be ready to sacrifice all your time, all your achievements, and all your bodies.

The Path of initiations that I teach is the Path of full humility before the Will of God, complete dedication and sacrifice.

There is no other Path, beloved, and our task is to direct you on this Path and to give your all the necessary ministration.

I AM Jesus,
and I have been speaking from
the highest point of Love towards each of you.

Your world is to be changed, and this change can only be implemented by way of transformation of your consciousness

May 28, 2005

I AM Jesus, having come to you today.

In my talk today I would like to focus on the information without which your advancement on the Path will be less successful. Therefore, you should find the time and get acquainted with this information.

You know that I stepped on Earth about 2000 years ago. That event had become so significant in the eyes of many people that a lot of them came to believe in me as a Son of God and their Savior. Their faith was the basis of the religion that you know as Christianity now.

But I must say that never during the entire history of existence did Christianity reflect the essence of the Teaching that I taught while living on Earth.

The last thing I want to do is to sow in your minds and hearts the seeds of distrust in Christianity or in any

51

other religion of the world. I just want to redirect your mind and attention from the external manifestation of my Teaching, as it is presented in all the outer Christian churches, towards its inner essence. This will help you to understand why I was crucified.

The inner essence of my Teaching was that this world is temporary and you must prepare yourselves for the transition into a new world — the Divine one — which is your true Home, whence you have come and to which you will come back.

Thus, you see that there is no religion in this world that reflects the essence of my Teaching.

The secret lies in the fact that any religion represents an interpretation of the Divine Truth in the minds of embodied people who try to formulate this Divine Truth in their own words. But as the consciousness of these people is far from perfection, the Truth that they present in the external religion is also far from the genuine Divine Truth.

That is why God has always sent Messengers and prophets to the world to remind you about the genuine Faith and about the true religion — based not on a cult or worshipping something outside you but on the adoration of the One within — inside your heart. It is a religion of the heart and it teaches you the universal Love towards the entire creation and the unity of all the particles of life.

Within this Faith or religion there is no place for a statement of superiority of one human over another. Within this Faith or religion everybody is in an absolutely equal state before the One God-Creator. Everybody is a servant in the Lord's temple.

As far as the human consciousness is imperfect, this imperfection has become the reason for inequality between people. The inequality in property has led to the division of humans into the propertied and the poor classes while the social inequality has led to the division of people into different social layers and castes. In its turn this has created unequal access for different layers of population to education, information, and various material possessions.

Any inequality, characteristic of your world, is a consequence of your imperfect consciousness. In reality all of you are absolutely equal before your Father. The Heavenly Father loves and cares about each of you in the same way.

However, due to the individual peculiarities inherent in you primordially, you yourselves create such karmic conditions that give birth to limitations. And in the course of time you find yourselves to be in different levels of evolution of your consciousness.

Some individuals receive an opportunity of a greater progress on the Path according to the merits that they had in their previous embodiments. Other individuals fall behind in their development and it is very difficult for their consciousness to master even the simplest knowledge.

That is why, beloved, God gives His blessing to such a large number of various beliefs and religions, even regardless of the fact that many of them distort the

Divine reality greatly. It is because for somebody such an approach is the best at the stage of evolution of his individual consciousness.

We are fully aware of the fact that the Dictations being given at present through this Messenger will be understood only by very few people. In many people, especially those who have firmly focused their consciousness on some religious doctrine, these Dictations will cause nothing but irritation and a wish to get even with the person through whom these Dictations are given.

And again you may find yourselves in the situation similar to that which humanity faced 2000 years ago when the enraged mob shouted, "Crucify him!"

Maybe this time the things will not come to a direct physical assault. But the negative forces that act in your world have taken care about making a whole arsenal of the ways for black magic and witchcraft to be accessible to those who so desire. Have a look at the shelves in your shops. Despite the abundance of books there, scarcely will you find a tenth of the books that are really necessary for your further spiritual unfolding. The remaining 90 percent of the books represent a spiritual surrogate, the reading of which is at best useless for you but at worst simply destroys your consciousness and your way of thinking and literally programs you to perform wrong actions.

This is why I always experience great joy while watching from the higher plane the next one to be found who got access to these Dictations, having discovered the websites they were located on in the chaos of the Internet. To me this person resembles a small light of reason, love, aspiration, and faith that suddenly flashes out in the darkness of your world.

I observe more and more such lights flashing out in the countries where people understand the Russian language in which these Dictations are given, and I regret that so far we have not managed to find reliable people through whom we could translate these Dictations into other world languages. That is why I ask those of you who might have a wish, an aspiration, and an opportunity to translate or to contribute to the translation of these Dictations into other world languages, please take the trouble to respond to my appeal and offer this important service to the world.

These Dictations are like a fresh breeze bursting into the stuffy atmosphere of the humans. For some people this fresh wind of change is useful, as they like to put themselves under its gusts in which they foresee fresh changes that are to come inevitably and that are already coming to the earth through the minds and hearts of those who read these Dictations. On the other hand, a lot of people will be so much irritated by this wind that they will want to stop up at any price this source of reformation and healing of the human consciousness. They will sense the danger coming from this source — the power that can destroy their usual way of life and make them adapt to a new world and to its transformed conditions of existence.

Just as it was 2000 years ago, they can make every effort to commit a physical assault on the source of Light or they can suppress it by their godless actions. However, recollect the Dictation given by Beloved Surya.[11] Everyone who undertakes any actions against our Messenger creates the direst type of karma of your world — the karma of godlessness.

Every person who visibly or within his consciousness flies in the face of God and His Law is like a cancer tumor that requires healing. But if this tumor is not curable, it requires an urgent surgery in order to save the Divine organism from it. This will be done and this is being done already for the benefit of the health of the entire organism of this universe, a part of which is this planet.

Your true enemies do not sit somewhere in the government and do not head any religion or faith. Your true enemies with whom you must lead a merciless fight are inside of you. And these are mainly your ignorance and your unwillingness to alter your consciousness.

You will look for thousands of reasons to justify all your actions, all your negative qualities, thoughts, and feelings instead of giving up everything imperfect and laying all your imperfections and attachments to this world on the altar of service to the true God who resides within you, within your heart.

I know that a day will come for each of you when the Light of reason will enlighten the darkness of your being and you will make your final choice. And in your

---

[11] Dictation "Never become adults in the questions of the Divine Truth cognition." Beloved Surya, March 9, 2005.

consciousness you will no longer separate yourself from God, a particle of who you are.

You will find the sense of your life and existence in the full submissiveness to the Will of God and in your service for the implementation of this Will in the surrounding reality.

Your world is to be changed and this change can only be implemented by way of transformation of your consciousness. This is the simple Truth that I came to teach 2000 years ago. But the people preferred to crucify me rather than alter their consciousness.

Well, you are again facing the same dilemma and you have to make your choice yet again.

That is why I wish you to make a right choice this time — to submit to the Will of God finally and to become His genuine servants for centuries.

I AM Jesus.

You must learn not to hold a grudge against your enemies

June 5, 2005

I AM Jesus, having come to you today.

Were you waiting for me? Do you want us to continue our Teaching and homilies?

There are a lot of temptations in your world, and amid the abundance of them it is very difficult for you to make a distinction between the true vibrations peculiar to our world and the lower vibrations inherent in the astral and mental planes. You should draw a sharp distinction because if you do not have in your consciousness a clear view of the direction to follow, you will delay your progress on the Path.

That is why the question arising before every person who reads the Dictations is the question of the authenticity of these Messages. I am fully aware of the difficulty you face. How can you in fact draw such a distinction?

You should pay attention to the informational component of the Messages. Does the informational part contain anything that goes against your inner guidelines? As long as the carnal mind of many of you is very strong, the easiest thing for you is, first of all, to analyze exactly the informational component. If you do not find any imperfections or chasms with your inner principles, then you may set about analyzing the next component of these Dictations.

Is there anything in these Dictations that is able to dishearten your free will? Is there anything in the Teaching we give through this Messenger that forces you to act in a certain way? Is there anything that makes you act out of tune with your interests? Please, just do not mix up your interests in the disciples standing on the Path with the interests of your ego. The interests of your ego are diametrically opposite to the interests of your Higher part. Consequently, it is exactly your inner contradiction that becomes the most persistent barrier to the perception of these Dictations. You begin to doubt and try to find a confirmation of the authenticity or the falseness of the source of these Dictations among your acquaintances and relations. But doing this you forget that everything depends on what is dominant in yourselves. If your ego and carnal mind dominate in you, you will sooner seek and find a confirmation to your opinion that the source of these Dictations is non-divine and that it is not worth heeding the information contained in them.

Your carnal mind is very inventive and nimble when it comes to the lessening of its dominant position within your being. It will make great efforts to find proofs confirming that these Dictations should not be read at all, since for your carnal mind the information and especially the energies contained in the Dictations are literally deathlike.

Only in the case when you are close to victory over your ego will you seek and find the confirmation of the authenticity of these Dictations. Eventually, the function of these Dictations, if they are read systematically, is to separate everything that is real from that which is false inside of you.

And when you get to the bottom of the question of the authenticity or the falseness of these Messages, you will actually either come into conflict with your ego or, on the contrary, indulge it.

However, you know that the main distinctive cue of every authentic Teaching is that it exactly reaches the aim of separating the real from the false within you and separating the grains from the weeds in your soul.

Thus, even if these Dictations are irritating and doubtful for you, there is no doubt that reading them will be of benefit for your soul. It is another matter that your unreal part tries and will continue to try to convince you to enter the fray with the source of these Dictations, and you will feel righteous anger within you and will do your best to cast aspersions on both the Messenger and her connection with our world. In this case you receive a certain sign, manifested in the physical plane in the form of your thoughts, feelings, and actions, that shows you better than any of our words and talks that there is something wrong with you and you need urgent help.

Any hostility and strong emotions that arise in you while reading these Dictations are signs for you — that you need urgent work upon yourself.

Thus, you have analyzed the informational component of the Dictations and understood with your external consciousness that they contain nothing unacceptable for you. But at the same time you keep feeling a negative reaction while reading them. This is evidence of the fact that a conflict has started within you — the separating of the real from the false within you. That means that the aim of the Dictations has been reached.

All you need is just to find courage and strength and try to rise above this situation so as to analyze it objectively, having elevated your consciousness and deafened your ego at least for a short time.

Those individuals who, after having analyzed the informational component of the Dictations and watched their reaction to reading them, did not find anything negative or causing a negative reaction, are fairly ready for the further progress on the path of discipleship. They are already either our disciples or quite ready to enter the rows of chelas of the Ascended Masters.

Thus, we have an opportunity to find our disciples, to establish connections with them with the help of these Dictations, and to work with our disciples who are in embodiment now.

One slightest hint given by us in the Dictations for perceptive and sensitive hearts is able to alter their angle of vision and to uncover before their prying glance and sincere spirit the things that were previously hidden behind the veil.

Therefore, nowadays, exactly as it was 2000 years ago, we are throwing the nets far and wide, and we have a chance to catch the souls who are ready to follow our Path.

Our disciples are able to make a distinction between the vibrations of the astral plane and the vibrations of the Highest Octaves. Our disciples can distinguish the requirement of the discipline necessary for them from the submission to the will of false teachers and false messengers.

Our disciples can make a distinction whether they receive energy while reading the Dictations or lose their energy.

I should tell you that when you feel negative emotions while reading these Dictations, you willingly give your energy to the forces of darkness.

That is why you are required to analyze attentively everything that takes place both within and outside you from the initial time of reading these Dictations.

You receive training, you receive knowledge through these Dictations, and you transform your consciousness just by reading them regularly and following the instructions given in them. Apart from all this, while reading these Dictations you receive an enormous amount of Light, and this Light, when you absorb it, is able to set against you the forces of darkness that exist in your environment. Every source of Light in your dense world irritates and provokes the dark forces to take active actions against such a source of Light.

And when the dark forces start attacking you from everywhere, do call to mind the Teaching I gave you 2000 years ago and just use the mightiest weapon of all times and peoples: "Whosoever shall smite thee on the left cheek, turn to him the other also."

You should love your enemies. You should bless your enemies. Your enemies give you a chance to get out of your karmic debts. Your enemies give you a chance to learn your lesson and to pass your test. I understand that in many situations it will be difficult for you to accept with humility and gratitude all the reproaches, attacks and threats aimed at you. But you must learn to take everything that falls to your lot with humility and submissiveness. You and only you decide how you can protect yourself with the help of your authorities and the structures called to settle disputes in conflict situations. But you must learn not to grudge your enemies. People who attack you, offend you, insult you, humiliate you are unhappy in their essence.

A man whose heart is an abode of God will never allow himself to do harm to another man.

Thus, all you can do when your enemies attack you is to forgive them and to pray for them, for they know not what they do. Their consciousness is clouded and sometimes completely seized by the dark forces, so that they are really not aware of their actions.

Only a person clouded with ignorance can give the dark forces a chance to perform wicked actions through him and to harm the blessed innocent ones.

It sometimes happens that God chooses you to draw the fire upon yourself and become a target for the dark forces that act through other people and use them for their malicious attacks. God chooses you to give you a test and simultaneously He contributes to the manifestation of the forces that in such a situation take off their hypocritical varnish and masks of piety and reveal their bestial grin.

Entrust yourself to the care of God. God cares for all His sheep. Be ready to sacrifice your body but to save your soul. The Truth is always in the places where the most elevated feelings reside among the wickedness of this world. Remember that you are responsible only for yourself and for your own reactions. No matter how unjust the treatment of other people can seem to you, forgive them.

Love your enemies because only your love and intercession can at times save the lives of these souls, possessed by ignorance and not knowing what they are doing.

Sometimes your prayer for your enemies allows the prevention of Divine justice and gives these souls one more chance to continue Life.

I was glad to give you this lesson once again. And I am ready to bend low before the souls of many of you because your suffering, troubles, and adversities sometimes surpass by far my Passion that I suffered on the Cross.

I AM Jesus.

A Teaching on healing

June 8, 2005

I AM Jesus, having come again.

By the established tradition, I will give a Teaching. Today the subject of our training is healing. You know that at the time of my incarnation 2000 years ago I successfully healed people many times. The fame about the miracles of my healing ran ahead of me. Wherever went there were always people who believed that I could heal them and there were people who did not believe in the miracle of healing.

Therefore, I always asked whether a person believed that he could be healed. I also asked whether a person wanted to be healed. At first sight these two starting points may seem to you to be insignificant and just clichés. However, it is exactly at these two midpoints that the key to healing is hidden.

Your consciousness must be ready to accept healing. If for some reasons your consciousness cannot believe that you can be healed, even God is not able to help you.

At the second midpoint you must want to be healed and you must ask for healing. If you do not ask for healing, even God is not able to help you because the inviolable law of free will governs in the universe.

There are a lot of reasons why you do not wish to be healed. One of the reasons is that your soul has willingly taken upon itself a disease as a burden in order to work off the karma of the world or your own heavy karma of the past. A lot of light-souls, while coming into embodiment, take upon themselves cruel diseases or congenital deformities so as to make a sacrifice for sins of the world through their suffering. With their external consciousness they do not realize the burden they have undertaken, but as a rule, such souls do not want to be healed and do not ask for it. And the only way of helping such souls is if their nearest and dearest beg for their healing because for them the suffering of a beloved one is an unendurable burden.

Thus, a person must believe in healing and ask for healing. Only if these two conditions are observed is it possible to start the healing. Every time before healing a person it is necessary to figure out the reasons for his disease. The Supreme Law can either allow you to heal a human or not to allow it.

Of course, in order to heal you should have the mantle of a healer that enables you to heal with the help of Divine mercy and Divine energy.

All the other sorts of healing are false practices when, with the help of ingenious manipulations, a healer transposes the negative energy that is the reason for the disease to another place or just temporarily stops the action of this energy.

The matters of healing are very delicate and serious ones. That is why I watch with concern the newly-sprung healers who experiment with the Divine energy at times without even having passed through the preliminary initiations that give them the right to work with the Divine energy that is the source of healing.

A lot of so-called healers do not have access to the source of the Divine energy at all, and all their manipulations, even if they bring temporary relief, in fact make the condition of a sick man graver.

Let me explain.

The reason for your diseases is the negative energy that accumulates in your aura as a result of wrong actions, thoughts, and feelings committed by you during this or previous lives. I am speaking now about the reasons for the diseases of the majority of humans, not about the cases when a person intentionally takes upon himself a disease as a burden.

This negative energy of yours that is the real reason for your disease and that has formed as a result of your wrong actions must be withdrawn out of your aura. After that you will be healed.

The Divine mercy necessary for your healing can be either shown to you or not. Everything depends on the heaviness of the karma that is the real reason for your disease.

For that reason, an empowering for the healing must be received from on high. As a rule, the people who claim to be healers do not have the proper level of initiations that allows them to know the Will of God in regard to each of the humans they try to heal. However, their wish to make money prompts them to replace the negative energy using certain manipulations that temporarily relieve the condition of a person. Some of the manipulations used in the process of such a healing create karma that will be too great a strain on such a healer. The shrewdest healers can even avoid the karma they create by such actions, but with this they make the karma of their patients much graver.

When the Supreme Law empowers a true healer to heal a human, the decision is based, as a rule, on the availability of good karma in this human, which can be used for his healing. Either this human himself or his soul must completely realize the wrongness of the actions that brought on the development of the disease, and he must firmly decide in his external consciousness never to repeat these actions in the future.

That is why after my healing I used to say, "Go and sin no more."

A true healer figures out the reasons for a disease very well and sees whom he can and whom he cannot help. The Divine energy is used for healing. A true healer withdraws the patient's negative energy and fills his aura with the pure Divine energy. This process may be conducted either mentally or by directly laying on of hands on the patient.

The essence of the healing is the exchange of the energies between the healer and the patient. The negative energy flows to the healer and the Divine energy flows to the patient. This process of energy exchange is regulated by the Supreme Law. In this case karma is not being created and real help is being given to the sick man. As a human who has the mantle of a healer must have passed through the major initiations before he was granted this mantle, the negative energy that he undertakes upon himself cannot harm him as a rule. The chakras of the healer transmute, transform, and burn dead all sorts of negative energy. Actually, the process of annihilation of the negative energy taken from the patient is analogous to the process that takes place when the spiritually advanced people transmute the world's karma undertaken by them.

The higher the level of spiritual merits of the healer, the faster is the process of transformation of the negative energies in his aura.

It goes without saying that if a person, after having been healed, still keeps performing the actions that were the reason for his disease, the disease will return in this or that form.

Thus, the healing of a man can take place only with his own help and with the help of his consciousness. The higher the level of consciousness of a man, the easier it is to help him. The healing is closely connected with the level of consciousness of the person.

The level of consciousness does not mean the development of intellect, speech, and carnal mind. Many simple people who have not had a good education sometimes possess a much higher level of consciousness than the people who received a first-class education and occupy high positions.

Each of you might have faced a necessity of applying to healers and psychics. And you have even applied to these healers. Maybe you have even received some healing of your ailments. But still you should be rather careful when applying to different healers and psychics, as many of them do not possess the spiritual merits that can empower them to heal in the name of God and with the help of the Divine energy.

But if your level of spiritual merits greatly exceeds that of the healer, a diametrically opposite process will take place during the séance of so-called healing. It is not the healer who will take upon himself your negative energy, but it is you who will take into your aura the negative energy from the aura of such a healer. And you will be lucky if you take upon yourself only the negative energy of this healer, and not that of all his patients whom he has healed in recent times.

You may judge indirectly the trueness of a healer by two things. First, a true healer heals your soul but not your body — that is, he helps you to reveal the reasons that caused your ailment. He shows you your imperfections that actually were the reason for the disease. And the second is that the gift of healing is a God-given gift, so a true healer will never take money from you for the healing. He received his gift for nothing and he must grant it for nothing. But you should never forget that you must pay back for the healing you received in one or another way. And always remember that it is in fact God who heals. A human-healer only entrusts himself to the disposal of the Higher Forces in order to serve the life and to relieve the suffering of people.

Today we have had a very important talk about healing. I think that each of you will gain the necessary benefit for yourself from this talk.

**I AM Jesus,
the healer of your souls.**

You cannot bargain with God

June 28, 2005

I AM Jesus, having come to you again.

Today I would like to touch upon a topic that can be of use to you but on which you can lay no stress by virtue of your devotion to the illusory world.

As always, your attention follows the things that surround you in the illusion. It is very difficult for you to raise your consciousness and to push yourself out onto that level of perception of the Divine reality when the entire surrounding world fades and pales in comparison with the beauty, feelings, and aspirations that you can obtain in our world.

However, your position in the dual world excellently contributes to your development and progress. There is a point on your Path that after having come through it, you will no longer be able to find satisfaction in anything surrounding you in the illusory world. And the main task for us and for you is to achieve this point on your Path. If you compare this with ascension onto a peak, you can picture yourselves climbing bare rocks, passing through crevasses, and suddenly coming to a mountaintop with a mesmerizing view that opens before your eyes. And it brings tears to your eyes and you realize that it was worth risking your life and overcoming yourself.

And you understand that your affection for the world you left gradually dissolves, and you merge with the beauty of this new surrounding world. And there is nothing to seduce you in the world you left forever, because in spite of the fact that you go on dwelling in the physical world, you no longer belong to it. There is already nothing in you from this world. There is no energy in you that can draw you back to the world of illusions. Nevertheless, you continue living in your world because you are fully aware of the fact that there are a lot of people who need your help and experience.

You see the reason for people's suffering, you see why they suffer, and you understand how they can get rid of their suffering. But, in spite of the fact that you speak to these people in very simple language and tell them very simple things, only a few of them are able to understand you.

I was on Earth, I spoke to people. I spent thousands of hours communicating with people. I tried to convince them of the things that I managed to realize after having wished to give up the unreal part of myself and having given it up. But, no matter how simply I tried to speak to people, there appeared to be only twelve disciples capable of developing a partial understanding of the Truth given by me.

Nowadays the same thing is happening. No matter how good and comprehensible the way of giving the knowledge is through this or any other Messenger, there are very few people who are able to absorb with their heart the essence of the Teaching given, and there are even fewer of those who wish to follow this Path.

We impart the Truth openly. Come up to our table. You can take everything to your heart's content. And the only payment that you need to make unavoidably is your unreal self, which you must freely sacrifice at the altar of the service to God, to Life, to the Hierarchy of the Forces of Light.

I can see as the hearts of many people reading these Dictations become enthusiastic about them. I see the flame of their aspiration flaring up. But it is so sad at times to watch a person reverting to the beaten track that is safe but leads nowhere except to death.

You are immortal spirits. It is sad to see you surrounding yourselves with unnecessary nonsense and trying to play at serving instead of serving sincerely.

How can you manage to combine nice words about God and Service with your life full of mercantile aspirations to a career, prosperity, and unconcerned idle dalliance?

You will not be allowed to combine these opposing things on and on. Sooner or later a moment will come when you will be obliged to make a choice whom to serve. Will you go on worshipping the golden calf of your world or choose the sincere service to God and Life?

I told you that it is impossible to be a servant of two lords. You cannot serve God and mammon simultaneously.

I said these words two thousand years ago. But up to these days each of you encounters the same choice in your life. God demands that you should devote yourselves to him. You cannot bargain with God. You cannot say, "Look, Lord, I am doing this for you, and now, Lord, it is your turn to do what I ask you for."

What great arrogance should one have to allow such a bargaining with God?

You come to the temple of God when you face blows and misfortunes, diseases and diversities. And all you come to the temple for is to arrange a settlement with God, to light a candle, and to ask for a trouble-free solution of your problems.

Do you seriously hope God will answer your request?

Are you really sure you can buy the Divine mercy for your sacrifices?

God needs no sacrifices of yours — neither calves you kill nor money. God wishes you to give up only one thing — the unreal part of yourself — the thing that is not from God in you.

This is so simple. But you cannot understand it for some reason. Every prophet or Teacher came to the world only in order to teach this Great Truth. And now you are receiving the very Truth that I preached 2000 years ago. You create perfect flying machines, you perform human space flights, you sink right to the bottom of the ocean, and you create state-of-the-art computers and systems of communication. You misdirect your mind towards the perfecting of the illusion. Why can you not understand this simple Divine Truth notwithstanding such a developed mind you have? It is because your mind is a carnal mind, a mind belonging to your world and serving your world. And your foremost task is to give up your carnal mind, to give up everything that binds you to your illusory world.

This does not mean that you should leave your home and go begging. Yet, even this can be beneficial for some people. You must remove from your consciousness all the attachments to your world. You can go on living in your world but only in order to give others a lead in passing the Path you have passed.

Each of you goes your own Path. But fundamentally only one Path can be considered to be true — the Path of the full refusal from your ego and from any attachment to your world. And the greatest sin is to try to make God serve you.

This is the very point where many souls lose their footing. You use the Divine energy for self-gratification of your ego instead of bending your knee to God and asking in humility, "Lord, here I am. Take me, use me. I am your slave. I am nothing, Lord, you are everything."

Think over the words I have told you today. These words may seem too stern to you or you may think that these words bear no relation to you.

Yet, do not jump to a hasty conclusion. Scrutinize your actions because these words are relevant to 99.99 percent of the people embodied now.

I have had to give you this strict homily because too many of you need exactly strict words that can take the gilt off your illusory world and remove the scales from your eyes. Only after that will you be able to see the Divine Truth finally and to strive for it with your whole being and with your whole heart.

I know that each of you will gain Victory and each of you will withstand and come off victorious from the skirmish with the illusion that has been lasting for millions of years already but the sands of which are running out. The world of illusions, in distinction from the Divine world, has its beginning and its end.

Hurry up on your Path to the real world. Do not wait for the gates of opportunities to shut in your face.

I AM Jesus.

Create selflessly, strive for the Divine world without looking back, and you will receive what you deserve.

December 20, 2005

I AM Jesus, and I have come to you through our Messenger. I have come again and like half a year ago I intend to give you the eternal Teaching on eternal life. Now I have come before Christmas, which is celebrated in the Christian world as a holiday honoring the day when I came into this world about 2000 years ago.

Then, as well as now, I am feeling the discomfort and the darkness of your world.

Oh, if you could only take a glimpse beyond the curtain out of the corner of your eye and feel the bliss of Heavenly life, I think that you would forever keep in your external consciousness the image that you should aspire to and that you must manifest in the life around you.

The whole problem of your consciousness is connected with its instability and lack of aspiration. You cannot manifest heavenly patterns in your earthly life until you gain that state of aspiration and highest faith, in which you will be able to dedicate all your earthly life to manifesting Divine plans in your physical octave. Only in this way you will be able to become the co-creator to God and manifest His Will for your octave.

Your world does not totally meet the requirements that it must satisfy at the given stage of evolutionary development. That is why the concern of the Ascended Hosts is so great, and that is why the nature of our Dictations has become so tough and uncompromising.

Believe that our love has not gone anywhere. We continue loving you as we have always loved you. But our love is manifested as caring about your souls' development and creating the conditions in which this development can be realized in the future.

Just as loving parents do not force their children to eat sweets all day long but vary their food so that they could grow healthy and active, the same way we try to provide you with the best spiritual food. And at the present time we are giving you the exact spiritual food that you need. And, even if it seems hard and not sweet to you, it does not mean that it is not good for you.

In our practice of teaching we constantly resort to alternating the carrot and stick method. When you get too much used to our affection and care, then we sometimes allow ourselves to show you that excessive care is not always useful. And the time comes when you must start acting on your own instead of expecting the whole Cosmos to continue spoon-feeding and cherishing you.

Had you not once in your life made the first step, you would have never learned to walk.

That first step for you is the realization of your responsibility not only for your life and the life of your family but also for the realization of your responsibility for the whole planet.

This is the next stage of the development of your consciousness. It would be unreasonable for you to continue relying on your nannies and parents when you have already reached that age at which you are capable of taking care of yourself. Moreover, you must assume the responsibility for the destiny of those livestreams that fell behind in their development and without your help are not capable of further development. And precisely the same role that we are playing in relation to you, the role of careful nannies and teachers, you must assume in relation to those representatives of mankind who are still playing childish games and do not wish to grow up.

From now on, education and upbringing of these unwise children lies with you as your duty and karmic responsibility. If you do not care about the younger generation and guiding those grown-up individuals who need your guardianship, then there is a high probability that too many livestreams on planet Earth will not touch the Divine Truth in this lifetime and will not be able to reach awareness of the eternal life.

I do hope for your care. When you choose to help other living beings, then you receive Heavens' help, and you receive the knowledge and the Divine energy that you need. If you do nothing, then you will not be able to fulfill your Divine plan and your Divine purpose, and you will not be able to help others.

This is a very ancient and wise law, and this law works impeccably. Never care for any reward that you expect to receive for your good deeds and help. Let God decide what you deserve. The more selfless your service is, the bigger the treasure that you save in Heaven will be.

And that is the very same choice and one and the same choice that you are making during your entire life. You either try to receive something tangible for yourself in the illusion surrounding you, or you think about the eternal life. Eventually you receive what your attention is focused on. And if from life to life you continue chasing the things of this world, then you are compelled to come to your world again and again and work off your attachments.

Therefore, create selflessly, strive for the Divine world without looking back, and you will receive that what you deserve.

I was glad to meet with you today, and I was glad to present you this short Teaching as a Christmas gift.

I hope that you will also remember me with love during these Christmas holidays and give me the love of your hearts.

I AM Jesus,
and I am standing in the flame of Love.

I am looking for heart-to-heart commune with those who are ready for such communication

July 8, 2006

I AM Jesus, having come to you today in order to give you my exhortations that I have prepared for you beforehand.

It is not often that we have an opportunity of immediate commune with those who are in embodiment now. However, this chance of direct communication between you and me is inherent in your nature. And if you took the trouble and aspired with all your heart, with all your soul to our commune, then you would be able to hear me. I would come to you exactly as I have now come to the body temple of Tatyana, and we would have a talk with you.

I could give you my exhortations directly, without a Messenger. And this is what I strongly desire — to have direct contact with each of you.

Most people who read these Dictations are familiar with Christianity, but religion is not an obstacle for the commune of ours. People themselves divided faith into different religions, and each religious system is trying to subordinate their congregation and is keeping vigilant watch so that they do not leave the bounds of their church. However, I exist and aspire to communication with everyone regardless of that religion to which you and your family belong. Do try to recognize me in your consciousness as an Ascended Master — not as an idol that is worshiped by most Christians of the world, but as your elder brother, your friend who is ready to respond to any request of yours and to come to the rescue when you are calling me.

I am that Master who is very close to humanity of Earth, and you cannot even imagine how close my presence is. I can be among you during your prayers when you are calling me. And I can come to you in the silence of your solitude when you sincerely intend to meet me and get some advice in a hard life situation. Do not hesitate to appeal to me. I am an Ascended Master and I have been serving humanity of Earth during all that time since I performed a transition in that life when I was Jesus. Since then, I have often come to those who have been practicing genuine Christianity in their hearts. But not to those who have made the religion of Christianity their source of living, and not to those who insincerely follow church dogmas and rules. I am looking for heart-to-heart commune with those who are ready for such communication. For many I am not so much a Christian symbol as a friend. And many incarnations ago I met you and gave you my Teaching during my incarnation as Jesus, and our connection still exists in the subtle plane. You have an opportunity to get your education in my retreat during your sleep. I am urging those of you who have not used this opportunity for our communication yet, to take advantage of this opportunity. If you are in a calm, harmonious state before your sleep, then after your prayer you can aspire with your thought toward our meeting, and we will surely meet during your night sleep. I will answer your questions and give you all possible help. Do not be confused by the fact that after you awaken you may not remember all the details of our meeting or even may not remember that our meeting has taken place at all. This is not important, because you will use the received advice in your life, even if it will go past your external consciousness. Therefore, keep the aspiration to meeting me within you and we will certainly meet.

Do not expect that I will come to you as if I were a human and dropped in to your place. No, our communication will take place in the subtle plane. And you should apply your efforts in order to hear me. I will speak to your soul or to your Higher Self. And you will hear my words in your heart. Those will not be common human words, and they may not even be thoughts. There will be the sense of my presence and your sense of my energy filling you. I will fill the chalice of your heart with life-giving water, and I will give you quietness and the sense of peace and bliss, everything that you lack in your life. And after you drink the nectar of bliss from my chalice, you will realize that everything that has concerned and tormented you, all your problems, moved somewhere aside. And many of them will not return to you, because

I have given you a part of my consciousness. And as your consciousness has changed, you will no longer be involved in those karmic situations that have caused your anxiety and trouble.

You are granted according to your faith. If your faith is strong and your aspiration cannot be broken by any life failure, then we will always meet with you. I have strong hopes that we will meet. For the opportunity of our meeting is that help for you that is given by Heavens.

Do not believe those who say that you need a mediator in order to communicate with me. No, I can have a meeting with you in the silence of your heart, and I will help you to solve your current problems. However, that degree of Faith and devotion that allows me to be present in your aura is not a common thing among people. I cannot come to you if you are staying in a big city and if you are too concerned about your earthly things and problems. I cannot come to you if you are burdened with any habits that separate us — by that I mean any of your attachments to alcohol, nicotine, watching TV, bad states of consciousness that haunt you: offence, envy, jealousy, and anger.

I will not be able to be present in your aura if you are burdened with these faults or any other faults, which you can easily list yourself because you know them pretty well and cannot get rid of them incarnation after incarnation.

I am open for communication but you must apply your efforts in order to approach me, raise your vibrations to that level where our communication can take place.

And each of you knows very well about those faults that impede your approach to me; however, you do not hasten to part from your faults and problems.

Well, I will wait until you become mature and decide to initiate immediate communication with me. For the time being I am having the opportunity to speak to you through this Messenger. And I also remind you of an opportunity to meet me in your dream.

The opportunity for our meeting always exists, and only you yourselves limit the opportunity of our communication.

And now I would like to wish you to acquire that inner aspiration that will surmount all your faults and will allow you to rise to the summit of the Divine consciousness without stopping or slipping down.

Sometimes one wrong choice of yours is enough in order to close the opportunity of our communication to the end of your current incarnation. Be careful as you go through life and consider every choice of yours and every step of yours.

There are a lot of inhabitants of the astral plane who aim to come in contact with you in order to get in your person to execute their will and their plans. And coming in contact and starting an interaction with such beings is much easier than coming in contact and having an interaction with me. For this you do not need to part from any of your habits.

Therefore, you will always know yourselves with whom you meet in the subtle plane. With me, or my counterpart, who is not from the Light. The key to the answer of this question will be the purity of your consciousness and those habits and attachments that you are not able to give up.

You do not even need to ask anyone about who you communicate with in the subtle plane. It is enough for you to simply make an unbiased analysis of your thoughts, your way of living, and your interactions with the people around you.

Therefore, everything is in your power, and you make a decision yourself concerning who you come in contact with in the subtle plane.

You need the gift of distinction, but sometimes you do not need any gift in order to make a distinction; you simply need to analyze your thinking, your habits, and your attachments.

I don't lose hope for meeting with you. And I look forward to our meeting.

I AM Jesus,
with great Love for you.

A Teaching on genuine Faith

January 8, 2007

I AM Jesus, having come to you today.

To make the purpose of my visit clear to you, I would like to dwell upon some well-known things that are accepted in your society at the current stage of its evolution. So, you live in your world and rarely come across the things that you should think about in the first place. You are concerned with everything that surrounds you in your life. You think about how to support your family, what to wear, or what to eat. There is much fuss in your life. It seems to you that you live quite reasonably, like everyone around you.

However, if you think about what you do in your lives and how reasonable it is from the viewpoint of the Teaching that I gave you 2000 years ago, nothing has changed. I may come into embodiment once again to tell you about the same things that I told you then.

Do you remember that I told you not to worry about daily bread, that the lilies of the field look much better than you do? The birds do not plow or sow, but they are fed. The Lord can take care of you in the same way.[12]

Being at the top of the evolutionary ladder of earthly evolutions, why are you paying so much attention to your most trivial needs? You literally make a cult of clothes, food, and prestigious things.

Nothing has changed since I came into embodiment 2000 years ago. You have mastered the usage of many modern things. You have advanced appliances, cars, and computers, but your consciousness is still on the same level as it was 2000 years ago. It is regrettable.

---

[12] Matthew 6:25-33:

25. "Therefore I say to you, do not worry about your life, what you will eat or drink; or about your body, what you will wear. Is not life more than food, and the body more than clothing?

26. Look at the birds of the air; they do not sow or reap or store away in barns, and yet your Heavenly Father feeds them. Are you not more valuable than they?

27. Can any one of you by worrying add a single cubit to your height?

28. "So why do you worry about clothing? Consider the lilies of the field. They do not labor or spin.

29. Yet I tell you that not even Solomon in all his splendor was dressed like one of these.

30. If that is how God clothes the grass of the field, which is here today and tomorrow is thrown into the fire, will He not much more clothe you—you of little faith?

31. Therefore, do not worry, saying, 'What shall we eat?' or 'What shall we drink?' or 'What shall we wear?'

32. For the pagans run after all these things, and your Heavenly Father knows that you need all these things.

33. But seek first the kingdom of God and His righteousness, and all these things will be given to you."

Do you understand where I am going with this? You are concerned about lots of unnecessary things that exist in your world, and you are busy with such things 99 percent of your time. Think about how you can come to your Heavenly Father if you are constantly busy with earthly problems.

Even when it seems to you that you dedicate yourselves to God, go to church, pray, and follow the rules of the church, even then you do not think about God as much as you are concerned with what other people think of you, how you look when you are in the church, and how other people look, those who are around you there. When I have a chance to be present in the church during a service — and I cannot be present at every service — I am surprised by your thoughts that I listen to and by your feelings that I sense. You know, it is very rare that you can find people who have truly Divine feelings. As a rule, you come to a temple to solve your earthly problems, to improve your life, and to ask that you and your relatives stay healthy. And sometimes, on the contrary, you even wish evil to other people that you know.

You continue solving your mundane affairs there in the church. You do not think about God. If you come up to my image, it is only in order to ask for something that you lack in your earthly life.

Think about my words. It can seem to you that I speak in riddles, and it is unclear what I am driving at.

I am talking about exactly the same things that I was talking about 2000 years ago. I am trying to make you understand that it is necessary to think about your soul, about your relationship with God, and about God within yourselves. I taught that you should be alone with God during your praying, and I condemned hypocrisy.[13] I revolted against the letter of the law; I made you think about the spirit. Now I am talking about the same things. Nothing but your relationship with God should interest you. And then, when you are searching for God in order to gain the meaning of life and begin to teach this meaning to others, you do not come to God, but you are only distancing yourself from Him.

Only when you find complete satisfaction in communication with God within you, and you do not need to share your quiet joy with anybody, because you are fully satisfied and happy, only then will you find true God. I am touched watching you, and you start feeling my presence.

I am always close to you. But your state of consciousness and your concern about earthly problems separate us from each other.

I am so keen to communicate with you! How rare are the moments when I manage to initiate direct conversation with some of you. I am so happy about these

---

[13] Matthew 6:5-6:

5. "And when you pray, do not be like the hypocrites, for they love to pray standing in the synagogues and on the street corners to be seen by others. Truly I say to you, they have received their reward.

6. But when you pray, go into your room, close the door and pray to your Father, who is unseen. Then your Father, who sees what is done in secret, will reward you."

moments. I am very much aware that every person who has had this experience of direct contact with me will no longer be able to live like all the rest. Such a person will seek solitude and inner communion with me. And then he will not be able to imagine himself and his life without this communion.

This quiet joy and serenity that such a person emanates in his life is better than any sermon or homily. He is a living example of a union with me and with God within him.

The best and most devoted Christians reached this inner union in the quiet of their hearts. However, there were others who tried to playact serenity, love, and grace. But one short glance cast at them was enough to determine the degree of their hypocrisy and to keep away.

I would like you to find the gift of recognition in your heart to identify all of the wolves in sheepskin, no matter what beautiful words they use in order to camouflage, no matter what they do. It seems that many people do the right things, talk about God, go to church; but in their hearts they are much farther away from me than many of those who do not parade their faith but fulfill the Father's commandments in their hearts.

I have come to you today to remind you about the Teaching that I gave 2000 years ago, and it has not lost its relevance. I would like to remind you that I was crucified for the Teaching that I had brought. And if I came today and started giving my Teaching, I would be subjected to the same persecution from scribes and Pharisees who occupy churches.

There are genuine servants, but there are even more false servants. That is why I want you to make a distinction in your consciousness not to condemn indiscriminately this or that church, this or that teaching.

The right Teaching may be incorrectly interpreted by unpurified human hearts, but it does not mean that the Teaching is wrong. First of all, seek God within yourself, in your heart. When you achieve inner harmony with God, you will not fear any wolves in sheepskin or any false pastors.

I was glad to come to you today to remind you about my Teaching that I gave earlier and that I bring again through this Messenger.

I AM Jesus.

A Teaching on the change of epochs

July 3, 2007

I AM Jesus, who has come to you.

Today, I am happy to give you another Teaching that you most likely know, but it is still necessary to remind you.

Human consciousness is so agile and it slips away from all our instructions so easily that we are persistently putting our efforts into returning you to your purpose, to urge you to remember your Source.

You came to this world millions of years ago. You have come to go through the necessary stages of evolution and gain priceless human experiences. When you began your path in the physical world, you were like little children. Now you have grown up. In the same way as little children who come into your world still remember their purpose, and then forget it when they reach maturity, you have also forgotten the purpose for which you came to this world. We come to call you back to the real world from where you have come.

This Truth that we have been teaching for millions of years is very simple, yet you expect something very complicated from us. Your mind is tirelessly seeking more and more of the new unresolvable tasks in your world. Your feelings are trying to find an equivalent in your world, to the most wonderful experiences that are typical in association with the Divine world.

You are seeking and continue to seek Truth in your world. However, I have come and I am telling you, "There is no Truth in your world." Your world has been created as a giant stage so that you can gain experiences and then leave this world of yours.

When you come to kindergarten, you take toys from the shelves and play with those toys. Later, when you grow up and leave the kindergarten, you no longer have interest in the toys with which you had played when you were children.

Now the time has come for you to leave earthly school and transition to a higher evolutionary stage of development. The imperfections with which mankind has burdened itself during its development are not characteristic of this stage. Therefore, only those of you who fully submit their lives to the Divine Law will be able to transition to that stage. When you are studying in earthly school, you are allowed to do different misdeeds for a certain period of time. Yet proper models are pointed out to you. There is a principle in pedagogics that an individual has acquired knowledge only when he or she is able to apply it in practice. Therefore, you are given an opportunity to acquire Divine knowledge and put it into practice.

There are people who are more successful in their acquisition of the Divine science, and there are those who have not been able to understand even its basics yet. Yet, all of you have to complete your earthly school. And each of you needs to demonstrate readiness for further learning.

We speak about proper models, about the models that are characteristic of the world in which you have to transition. You cannot transfer to the next grade until you have learned the lessons of the previous grade. Therefore, you are required to manifest the qualities that are typical of the Divine world. You have to gradually give up the manifestation of any negative qualities that you have acquired throughout your earthly evolution. The substitution of the old and the outdated with the new can only be made by you yourselves, by making choices in your life.

Everything has gotten mixed up in your life — the good and the bad, the Divine and non-divine. Only you yourselves can clean up your world by abandoning non-divine manifestations and aspiring to Divinity. We cannot do it for you. We can give recommendations and provide our Teaching, but you yourselves have to solidify your theoretical knowledge in practice.

Do not think that you have a lot of time. The situation in your world is worsening every day. The vibrations of the physical plane are rising involuntarily, and you get into challenging conditions where you are trying to return to the behavioral stereotypes that you are used to, but everything that had previously brought you pleasure no longer attracts you. You cannot understand why the things that used to be pleasant for you do not bring you the same satisfaction. You continue to follow old behavioral stereotypes in your life, but you understand that they have lost their meaning.

You need to follow the rising vibrations of the physical plane in your behavior; otherwise you will fall out of space and time and will not be able to continue your evolution.

From now on, everything that is capable of elevating your consciousness will bring you satisfaction. Everything that lowers vibrations will cause aversion and rejection.

Of course, not all people are able to realize what is happening. However, for the majority of people it is becoming clear already that neither alcohol, nor music that is destructive to the surrounding environment, nor past hobbies give them satisfaction. The search for something new is becoming wider and wider.

You are given recommendations on how to protect yourselves from the influence of everything that brings low vibrations. When you are able to bring the Divine models into your life, you will be able to feel fulfillment and harmony. Of course, not all people are able to strive for the proper models. That is a natural and legitimate stage at which there will simultaneously be people with such different levels of vibrations, that when they meet each other in the street, they will perceive each other as aliens.

The mix of the good and the bad on Earth has to be sorted gradually. The process of sifting out the ashes from cinders is taking place in the Divine thresher.

And you are living now, during this time. That is why it is very difficult for you. However, this process has a beginning and an end, as does everything in the physical world.

It is a necessary process that at first small areas will form on Earth where people with this new consciousness and new way of thinking will live; and then there will be more and more areas of this kind. Gradually, Earth will become free of the places around the world where low vibrations prevail. With time, water and fire will wipe off all such places on Earth, where the bearers of old thinking and low vibrations are concentrated.

New places on Earth will be available for the representatives of the new race, who are starting to come on the planet already.

Now is a very difficult time when literally every person considerably changes the situation on planet Earth with his or her choices.

We give you our support and our help. There has never been such a close collaboration between your world and the world of the Ascended Masters. We are waiting for the situation on Earth to change to such an extent that we will finally be able to come visit you and give our instruction directly, avoiding intermediaries. You yourselves are creating such conditions for us now by changing your consciousness and trying on new garments, pure garments woven from your perfect thoughts and feelings.

I have come to you as a representative of your elder brothers who have finished earthly school and are waiting for you at the Higher planes of Existence.

I AM your elder brother, Jesus.

Instructions for every day

December 31, 2007

I AM Jesus, beloved by you. I have come to renew our relationship based on mutual love. You love me, don't you?

I visited Earth 2000 years ago. And one of the aims of my coming was to give the humanity of Earth an example of love — not of the love based on the fleshly desire but of the love based on a more elevated Divine feeling.

I spoke about it, and I taught my students about the relationships founded on this feeling of love. The relationships based on the mutual feelings of love are the only necessary conditions when a community — several people or families — gather to live together.

It is difficult for you to understand this feeling that one feels toward all people without exception. However, I had this gift. God gave me this ability: to Love all people. It is thanks to this ability that I was able to withstand all the ordeals that God sent to me.

Only with the feeling of unconditional, infinite Love are you able to build true relations in your world.

You are used to feeling love for your parents, for men and women, and for children. All of these are different manifestations of one and the same Divine Love. But these are only small manifestations, narrow ones. I am telling you about greater Love, about the Love that does not differentiate men, women, children, animals, and even inanimate nature.

I am telling you about the Love that expands boundlessly and includes the whole Creation, everything that surrounds you.

It is very hard to feel such Love in your world. However, if you do not learn to love in this way, you will not be able to move along the Path of evolutionary development that we are teaching you.

The Ascended Masters, who direct the evolutions of the planet Earth, all possess this quality of Love in varying degrees. Believe me, if we did not feel tremendous all-embracing Love toward you, we simply could not have managed to endure those millions of years during which we have been working with the humankind of planet Earth. We feel Love toward you not because you are so good but because you are part of God. There is an undeveloped particle of God in every one of you, and the task for each of you is to manifest God and to give God the opportunity to act through you.

Now you are too preoccupied and anxious about your worldly affairs. You are constantly in a hurry, and you are toiling over the fulfillment of large and small tasks of life. The time will come when you will be able to discern a more global picture of the development of human civilization behind the whole fuss of life. You will learn to watch and see how every life situation that arises before your sight has causes that come into action from what you alone have created earlier. You will learn to distinguish causes from effects. Gradually you will be able to unravel the tapestry of Life and to see the reality that exists behind it. You will be able to discern the real world of God.

For now, you have much to learn and a lot that you have yet to understand.

The only thing I would insist on is not to stop aspiring upward in your development to the Divine reality. You should not forget that there are bigger tasks behind all small things in life. The more successfully you fulfill all the tasks facing you during the day, the sooner you will learn to see and to know familiar situations behind the whole complexity of life. You will be able to see the cause of troubles and misfortunes, to see it yourselves and tell others about it.

You have everything in front of you. You will be capable of assuming more responsible service when you fully master life in your physical octave. We cannot entrust you with many practices and techniques, and we cannot assign to you the management of the energy in the matter until we are sure that you have reached the age when you can have a responsible attitude toward the errands given to you, and that you can use the knowledge correctly.

Until then, you will continue staying in illusion. You yourselves determine all of your own development and its pace. For some, this development goes very quickly and successfully, accomplishing everything in one lifetime, while others cannot work off a single quality or a single shortcoming during their whole lives. It seems sometimes that many animals are much quicker-witted than some representatives of the so-called reasonable humanity. Indeed, your reliance on the arm of flesh, your desire to control hurricanes and earthquakes makes us smile. You will not be able to pacify the elements outside of yourselves until you learn to confine the storm of emotions inside of you.

When you "lose your temper" and experience a state of utmost imbalance, remember then that as recently as last week, you were trying to balance a particular situation on planet Earth. God shows you the level of your achievements.

Only the person who has reached complete humility is able to remember God in the most undesirable and unfavorable situations, and only such a person gets our attention and we are ready to work with him or her.

Keep the correct state of consciousness during the whole day, day after day, year after year, and you will reap an unprecedented harvest of your spiritual attainments.

I have visited you to give you some instructions. I hope that these instructions of mine will not drive you into despair. You should not reproach and reprimand yourselves for the past mistakes. It is very important to give an appraisal of every deed in your consciousness

— even the most terrible one — to repent in your heart, to make a decision never to allow such a deed again, and after this to never give thoughts to this deed again.

For when you return in your thoughts to this or that unseemly situation over and over again, you constantly feed it with your energy, and as a result you grow a frightful monster that you cannot cope with alone without our help.

I came and now I leave. It is a pity for me to part with you, but the time of our talk has run out.

I AM Jesus,
your brother and helper on the Path.

The internal and external Teaching

June 25, 2008

I AM Jesus, who has come to you. I have come, as last time, in order to give you certain instruction that I hope will be useful for your souls. There are an external and an internal Teaching. You know about them, or you may have heard about them. What is the difference between the two?

Every time when we provide instruction to you on this topic, we present the material slightly differently so that you can absorb it in its fullest. You know that I gave my Teaching to many people when I was incarnated 2,000 years ago. Was that Teaching the external or the internal one? In order to answer that question, let us speculate together.

When a messenger or a prophet comes into incarnation, he or she comes with a certain goal or mission. Such a herald always has only one mission: to restore the true Teaching, the Teaching that had always existed in the world since the beginning of ages but

106

was forgotten many millennia ago. You need to have the knowledge refreshed. That is why we come today in order to give you refreshed knowledge, the knowledge that you can understand now.

At the time when I was incarnated, and even much later after that, if there appeared a person who carried the Teaching that we are widely giving now, he would not be able to preach so widely and openly simply because there were many limitations that are peculiar to all world religions. Each religion is a set of certain dogmas and rules. You can probably guess that the majority of these dogmas and rules were not given by me or the founders of other religions, but they evolved much later and were introduced by the church fathers. That is because each person is willing to instruct others in the best way possible based on his worldview and culture in general. However, when this person does not speak in the name of God, but his carnal mind speaks for him, the result of his efforts is sometimes directly the opposite of the result that the Ascended Hosts wish to see manifested among people. Namely, everyone is striving to find in all truly existing sacraments an explanation that will be appropriate for the human mind. What cannot be explained is either silenced or proclaimed as God's miracle. When many generations of people repeat and pass on the miracle that had been performed many hundreds or thousands of years ago, a stereotype or a dogma is formed. That dogma begins to exist independently from the consciousness of those people who joined a certain religion or church.

There is Truth in every dogma, but for that Truth to become comprehensible for new generations of people, there must be a person who will come and refresh the human understanding of the Divine Truth again.

It has always been this way. It is similar to how you dig a well and draw water from it. You get used to drinking water from that well because there is no other source of water available to you. Even when, with time, the water becomes stale, you put up with the stale condition of the water because you do not know how to discover a new water source. Then a new person comes who digs a new well. With caution, you taste the water from it because you understand that water can be different, and you may even get poisoned from it. Only after a significant amount of time, all residents become used to the new well and begin to draw water from it.

In the same way, a new Teaching is given. Every time, a new person comes and brings the same ancient Teaching that is understood by his contemporaries. In the beginning, this Teaching contains absolute Divine vibrations and attracts everyone with its novelty. Yet, after the bearer of the Teaching leaves, the disciples who accepted the Teaching begin to interpret it in their own ways. That is because the stream of Divine opportunity gets cut off, and there is no human on Earth who would be the conductor of the Divine energy.

Every time, the same Teaching is given, and the essence of that Teaching is simple and clear even to an infant. Yet, what an infant can understand escapes the carnal mind and cannot be logically analyzed. That is why it will be very important for each of you to find the source of the Teaching within you. All true religions are based on the teaching about God who resides in the heart of every person. Because people have lost the ability to hear God in their hearts, there are now mediums that hear God or say that they hear God.

There is nothing bad about coming to an intermediary for help so that he can show you the way. The only issue is to what extent that medium is the bearer of the Divine Truth. That is why it is easier and more effective if each of you can attune to the Divine tune and feel the Divine vibrations in your heart. Believe me, God lives in the heart of each of you. You do not need to run around Earth searching for someone to guide you. However, because many people who are living now have lost the ability to hear God directly, you must at least have the criteria that will allow you to uncover wolves in sheep's clothing among the old and new preachers.

Where there is God, there is no room for tattles and gossip. Where there is God, there is no room for opportunistic interests and desires. Where there is God, there is only giving — you are being given, again and again, the Divine nectar and are not asked for anything in return.

Never chase external rituals. Never try to find sacraments where there are none. Live simply. Follow the commandments given by Moses and the prophets, and first and foremost, try to maintain in your heart the feeling of Love and compassion toward your neighbor and all living beings.

The way you treat every particle of Life, the way you treat any Divine manifestation will distinguish a true believer from a hypocrite who covers up by the name of God but does not have God in his heart.

I gave you the commandment "Love each other." I have come in order to tell you that when Love lives in your heart, you do not need any external preacher; you do not need to spend your time searching for God outside of yourselves, because you have Love and therefore, you reside in God because God is Love.

I have come to you today in order to give you understanding of the internal Teaching that resides in your hearts and that is Love.

I AM Jesus.

Truth, God, and Love abide inside you

January 3, 2009

I AM Jesus, who has come to give you spiritual instructions.

I have come this day to dispel some of your views and beliefs about me and the Teaching that I brought to the world 2000 years ago.

By cosmic measures, it has been a very short time since the time that my Teaching was given. However, misrepresentations made by many people distorted the original sense so much that even I can hardly guess the correct meaning of the phrases recorded in the Gospels.

My Message was much broader than the interpretation my disciples were able to grasp and record. Subsequent editors kept distorting the text continuously. Many of them sincerely intended to convey the contents in a better way, naturally, to their understanding. Many provisions of the Teaching given by me totally did not fit with other peoples' concepts, and they were silently deleted. That is why just three hundred years after my leaving the physical plane you received the Teaching only remotely resembling the true Teaching given by me. For comparison I can provide an example of a candle and the sun. That is the proportion of the essence of my Teaching in the present Christianity.

But the foundation was laid. And the Divine opportunity, provided through me, contributed the viability of the Teaching, in which many seeking hearts for many hundreds of years found soothing and peaceful for themselves. Goodness of the Teaching was passed not so much through the Gospel texts as through those objects and images that we saturated with our presence. Then my and Mother Mary's images in icons were revived.

Through our images, many seekers could directly connect to our presence and get the Divine Grace directly by using our images as conductors on the physical plane.

The elders who left for hermitages to look for God found Him in the quietness of their hearts. And Grace, an invariable accompaniment of Divine Revelations, visited them in the darkest winter evenings and nights.

The dawn of their consciousness made it possible to keep fundamentals of our Teaching in people's minds for many centuries. These fundamentals were passed on directly from the elders' hearts to the hearts of those who came to them seeking soothing for their souls.

Many people in the world were sick in their hearts. And now many people are yearning for a genuine Faith, and many need help.

We are using any focus on the physical plane to show our presence and to provide soothing for hearts grieving so much and feeling deprivation and misery in the absence of the true Faith so sharply, that the Divine opportunity opens up for them in Mother Mary's smile or in the crackle of a candle in church.

When we are able, we give the maximum of possibilities to the curious ones. We are not disturbed by either Teaching distortions or church rites. We can stretch out a helping hand to hearts needing our help through all of it.

Many people come to church and we sooth them. Other people are looking for a special path of their own beyond the church, and we are also soothing them.

No matter which path people follow, what matters is the quality of their hearts and the degree of their Faith. They will find us even in a desert.

The worst thing is when people lose faith or begin to use the Divine aspiration of others to receive something for themselves or to attain private goals.

When I came to Earth, I spoke exactly about that. I spoke about the hypocrisy of scribes and Pharisees who were involved in shady deeds under the cover of noble appearance and sly terms from scriptures, and who rubbed their hands in the evenings with joy because they had managed to snatch another large sum from innocent sheep.

I, along with all Messengers of God, rose against hypocrisy at all times. The Divine Truth is simple. Divine

Love is open to all. Everything is on the surface, and you do not need to pay money for the Divine Wisdom. God gives everything to everybody for free.

You just need to find a narrow path leading you to the Divine Summit among thousands of roads and highways leading to dead ends.

You need to realize that the true faith has nothing to do with rites and ceremonies. True Faith is in your hearts. And God lives in your hearts. For people who perceive the true God dwelling in their hearts, it makes no difference what temple they go to for prayer.

It does not matter whether you go to a Buddhist pagoda, to a Christian church, to a synagogue, to a mosque, or to a prayer house. If you go there to find God, you will find God everywhere.

If you are going there with an empty heart, you will not find God anywhere.

The mechanical repetition of rituals and prayers without sincerity and inner Faith will not do any good for you. You can pray for a thousand years, but if while doing so you continue to seek harm for your neighbor, then your prayers and your efforts are not worth ten cents.

No Faith can justify the crime you commit in the name of God.

I ask you to consider my words today. I am compassionate to those who are seeking God and are unable to find Him. And there are quite a number of people who use their sincere impulses for their own good.

The whole root of the problem of faith resides within your hearts. You can find absolutely faithful and devoted votaries of God in any religion of the world. You can also find those who under the pretense of serving God, serve their egos, the devil who took hold of their hearts, in any religion too.

I have come to remind you that Truth, God, and Love abide not beyond you — they abide inside of you. We will help you to discover these riches in your hearts. Ask us for help. Turn to us with calls and prayers. A sincere call can reach any Master, and we cannot fail to respond to you since we regard answering a call as our duty, and this duty is sacred for us.

I AM Jesus.

Why everyone cannot follow the Path

June 26, 2009

I AM Jesus.

I have come to you. You work hard in your world. You are constantly residing in an environment that is not dignified for mankind. You have gotten used to the stench. Now after a long wait, the time is coming when a new consciousness must appear amidst all your chaos and hustle and bustle. The advent of this consciousness is unobservable, but the new consciousness must inevitably come to your world. And there are enough volunteers who have expressed a desire to go along my Path and to undergo a crucifixion in the material world as a reward for their devotion and service.

Yes, in your world there is no reward and there cannot be any reward for your service or for the spiritual feat that you are bearing, which is similar to the cross that I carried to Calvary. And those of you who wish to receive fame, recognition, honors, or money and who are ready to do the necessary work for the Masters for the sake of getting all this — your hour has not yet come. You will not be able to go along my Path.

For you to be able to step onto the Path of Christ, you need to make this decision within your hearts. And I will render my assistance and lend my support to each of you who wants to follow my Path sincerely within your heart. But you need to realize that there is no way back from this Path. You must realize the entire responsibility for going on the Path of Christ. You cannot wish to follow the Path of Christ today and then tomorrow leave your cross in the attic and continue enjoying the pleasures of your world.

You make the choice inside yourself. And you must weigh thoroughly how strong your aspiration is. Many people decide to follow the Path in the first flush of enthusiasm and under the influence of their mood. But after a day or two, their determination evaporates. New pleasures overtake their being and they forget about the decision they made. However, for you it means a big step back. Every time the Ascended Hosts hear your sincere call, a mechanism is activated that makes you return onto the Path. You forget in the hustle and bustle of your everyday life that you made a commitment to follow the Path of Christ. However, all the conditions around you intensify and you enter a period of temptations and tests. And as you forget about your decision, every new test engenders discontent and fear within you. You start making appeals to God asking Him to lend you a helping hand in passing this dark period of your life.

Now imagine yourselves in the place of the Ascended Masters. How would you react if today you were asked for one thing, but tomorrow for something completely opposite?

117

Inconsistency, mood swings, and dependence on the surrounding environment are literally the scourge of your time.

You should develop in yourselves the basic qualities of a disciple: consistency, discipline, devotion, humility.

If you do not develop these qualities in yourselves, then you will not be able to progress on the Path of discipleship, and you will drop out of sight of the Ascended Teachers of humanity because we will not be able to trace you amidst the chaotic flashes that we observe among mankind from our ascended state of consciousness.

Imagine a lighthouse that works today and does not work tomorrow. We focus on the burning fire of your hearts. When the fire on the altar of your heart keeps burning day and night without interruption and its brightness is smooth despite all the obstacles and ills of life then angels can always distinguish you in the twilight of your world and give you help and support.

The main and basic obstacle that we encounter among embodied humanity is volatility and the inability to be consistent in everything. Therefore, instead of feeling discontent and expressing displeasure to the Ascended Hosts, try to develop the basic qualities necessary for you on the Path.

At all times, the qualities of constancy and persistence in achieving objectives have been highly recognized.

You need to maintain your aspiration, and then the burning flame on the altar of your heart will be uniform, and we will know that now this individual is ready for us to begin our work with him.

We consider not only the present moment; we are also perusing the Akashic records.[14] And we can judge how many times this individual decided to go on the Path of Initiations and how many times he swerved from the Path. That is why each of you has your own waiting period for a Teacher who will come and get in touch with you. We see at a glance when you manifest the smooth burning flames in your hearts, but at times the Akashic records show that you started to follow the Path a few dozen times but went off course. And then we are not allowed to work with you until the end of the current embodiment. However, this does not mean that you do not need to show readiness to follow the Path, because your aspiration and constancy will undoubtedly generate the momentum that will be needed in your next embodiment. This explains why some people can easily master our Teaching, being light on their feet and ready to gather and go where we point at our first call. Yet, other people read the Teaching and listen to the Dictations, but at the next moment they are already fascinated by something else, and they thrust aside the books of our Teaching and run toward another trinket or nonsense of their world.

---

[14] Akashic Records are the information field of the universe, in which all the events of the past, present, and conceivable future are fixed.

Each of you is at your own level of consciousness. Since you live at the time of Kali Yuga,[15] very few individuals who have certain spiritual achievements are left in embodiment at your time. Others are given a chance to go through re-education. And many of you go through this re-education for many embodiments. An opportunity is given to you again and again before the passage of the Divine opportunity closes. And when you pass away and appear before the Karmic Board, you see your mistakes in horror and beg for one more opportunity and for one more embodiment. The mercy of Heaven truly knows no bounds. And each of those who plead is given a new chance. But with every new embodiment, the conditions become more complicated. Your karma becomes denser and it is more and more difficult for you

---

[15] Yuga in Hinduism denotes a world period or cycle. One cycle is Maha Yuga (4,320,000 years), which consists of four smaller Yugas: Satya Yuga, Dwapara Yuga, Treta Yuga, and Kali Yuga. The ratio of their duration is 4:3:2:1. The first one is Satya Yuga, or the Golden Age. It is characterized by righteousness, abundance, and widespread spiritual culture. People living during this age have the most elevated qualities, supernatural abilities, great strength and intellect, and they are very tall and beautiful. The second age is Dwapara Yuga. During this time, the piety of people is reduced, and the first signs of degradation in the society appear. During Treta Yuga, piety is reduced even more, although people still have a very elevated nature and they are very strong. The last age, Kali Yuga, is called the Iron Age, or the Age of machinery. It is the shortest one (432,000 years), and is the darkest of all four. This epoch is characterized by the widespread fall of morality. General economic and spiritual degradation develops. Kali Yuga is the age in which we live. However, it will eventually come to an end with the coming of the Golden Age. (From the Encyclopedia of Esotericism.)

to get out of the viscous treacle of imperfect thoughts and feelings in which the physical world lives for the most part.

Therefore, before complaining about your unhappy lot and asking to be released from your karmic burden or to make it less burdensome, remember that you yourselves have earned in your previous lives everything around you and everything happening to you now. That is why sincere repentance and confession sometimes ease your karmic burden by half. God does not want you to suffer; it is you who devote yourselves to misery. The understanding of your mistakes and the penitence give almost an immediate alleviation of your condition, and the burden lying on your shoulders lightens.

Today I have given you a Teaching on the Path and on why not everyone among you can follow this Path in this life.

I AM Jesus.

The Essence of the Rose Path

December 11, 2009

I AM Jesus, having come to you.

So much effort was spent by the Heavenly Hosts to make this Message of mine possible. Now, I am with you.

Are you glad about our meeting? I suppose that most of you had some doubts regarding the possibility that I can give this Message and to what extent this Message truly belongs to me, beloved Jesus.

I will resolve your doubts. Do not think about the source of the Message; do not think about how it has appeared in your world. Concentrate your attention on the Message itself and try to read it with your heart — not with your mind, but with your heart. Your mind and your heart are not always in agreement. It is your mind, your carnal mind that is mostly preventing you when your heart calls you Heavenward.

Your mind tells you that this is impossible; it finds thousands of reasons not to change anything in your life. And most often you follow your mind, not your heart. The voice of your heart gradually becomes quieter and quieter, and it finally subsides completely. And then, when you have had enough running from pillar to post in your life, have faced many obstacles, and have unhealable wounds in your subtle bodies as well as psychological problems, you hear somewhere or remember that it would be good to seek help from your heart.

However, during the long years of living without God, your heart has been covered with such warts and scabs that it cannot answer your calls.

You are puzzled because you ask for help, you really need help, and you cannot get it. Your heart keeps silent.

At such moments, many people sink into despair or lose hope and fall into the worst states of consciousness.

You should not do that, beloved. Your heart hears you, but you cannot hear it because you yourself have covered it with a shell. You have met many life situations that hurt your heart, and you hardened your heart. This means that your heart was getting covered with armor, a shell, behind which it was hiding from blows, severe blows that you faced in life. Therefore, step by step you need to dissolve this shell, this armor that your heart is covered in. You will not be able to dissolve this shell at once, nor even in a month. A much longer period of time may be necessary. It may even take the same amount of time as when you were ignoring your heart.

However, in order for you to return to the true Life — not to that life that surrounds you but to the real Life, eternal Life, which is awaiting you — you need to move forward, step by step without stopping, and to remove one cover after another from your heart.

There was much evil that you encountered in life. There were a lot of things that used to make your heart die within you. Talk to your heart and feel the warmth within it. Imagine that you are breathing with your heart. Talking with your heart must become your daily practice.

As you devote more and more attention to your heart, it will respond to you. And there will come a moment in your life when you will hear the voice of your heart in the depth of your being. It will be a very tender and gentle voice. You need to try not to lose this voice amidst the surrounding hustle and bustle. You need to try very hard to hear what your heart is telling you.

If you manage to do so once and then a second time, you can be congratulated on a great victory!

You have returned to the true, Divine essence that exists within you. And in comparison with the tenderness, warmth, Love, and bliss that reside within you, inside your being, all the entertainment of your world appears to be vulgar and pointless. You will acquire a more exquisite taste, and you will become familiar with the joys of the Divine world.

When this occurs within you, you will be able to say to yourself, "That is done! I have overcome the unreal part of myself. I did it!"

However, just when you discover the peace and serenity inside your being, the rest of the world will turn against you.

I will not reveal any secret here. This story is as old as the hills. When your vibrations rise, you become a source of danger for the surrounding world because people in the rest of the world continue to shelter their hearts behind an impenetrable shell, and they do not wish to respond to the Love that is streaming through your being.

What should you do in this situation? Heed the voice of your heart. Your heart will tell you what to do. As a rule, the circumstances of your life and your karma do not allow you to escape from the grip of the world. You are compelled to remain in the world as a sacrificial Lamb of God. You are forced sacrifice yourself in order to give the thirsty a drink with your blood. And when tormenting you and sucking your blood, the world may stop for a while and think about the fact that God is inside every being. And this God is waiting for the proper moment to speak to every person living in this world.

There are too few awakened souls in the world now. Therefore, the fate of these souls is to be sacrificial Lambs of God in the world.

This will continue until a sufficient number of such souls manage to unite and create such a momentum of Light that it will outweigh the entire darkness of the world.

Until that time, the fate of each Christ-being is to be a victim of the world, just like I made my sacrifice and was crucified on the cross of matter in my time.

I have revealed the essence of the Rose Path to you. I have taught you the essence of the Path that

I followed during my incarnation 2000 years ago. Since that time, many souls of Light have followed my Path. You know some of them because they went down in history as saints and prophets. Others are unknown to you because the essence of the Path is to sacrifice yourself for the sake of saving the world. And when that happens, it is not spoken about on every street corner.

Today I have given you a view of the Inner Path that you are being taught by the Ascended Masters.

I AM Jesus.

A Talk about the incarnation of the Masters and the institution of Messengers

January 6, 2010

I AM Jesus.

I have come to you, to those who are waiting for me to come and who love me. I know, beloved, that for those people who have chosen my Path, the surrounding world is dark and dense. I know that no matter where you go, you feel like foreigners. You are not of this world. That is because you have made your choice in favor of the Divine world. And your Service to the world is similar to the Service that I rendered.

When you can attune yourselves to me, to my vibrations, I can come into your world through you for a short time. But I thank God for this opportunity to see your world. It happens so rarely. And it is necessary for me. For through you, as in the past it happened through me, God has an opportunity to look into your world.

I am talking to you as if you understood me. However, the majority of people cannot understand why the mighty Masters cannot come in to your world.

Unfortunately, it is so, beloved. Only very seldom and for a very short period of time can we be present in your world. It also happens when there is a vessel who is ready for Service and who is prepared to the extent that one of the Masters or I can dwell in your temple for some time.

The rest of the time the veil is so dense that the direct presence is impossible, even to a small extent.

We can create an impression about your world based on the Akashic Records or based on what you tell us when you come to the etheric retreats of the Brotherhood during your sleep or after your transition.

I am telling you this so that you can understand your responsibility for your world. Only an incarnated person can act in your world. And we can act through an incarnated person only when he has completely devoted himself to the Will of God and has voluntarily chosen to devote all his life to the Service.

It seems simple, beloved. In fact, the aura of each of you contains a lot of negative energy, the so-called karma that has not been worked off.

When you make a sincere and firm intention in your heart to Serve the Brotherhood, you step onto the Path of Initiations. At least seven years should pass before you can truly fulfill certain tasks of the Brotherhood. And during these seven years and more, depending on your position on the Path, you prove your ability to serve the Brotherhood every day. Every day a certain karmic energy rises in you in order to be worked off. And you must demonstrate your ability to cope with each manifestation of imperfection that is present in you.

Beloved, there are no perfect people among those who are incarnated. If you were perfect, even to a small extent, you would not be able to be present in your world. For now it is the darkest hour on the planet.

During this time, not a single Master can be incarnated. We make attempts of partial incarnations. However, in order to make the presence in your world possible for us, we must align our vibrations with your world. And for that, similar to a diver who takes a heavy stone to sink down to the bottom, we also burden ourselves with karma so that our vibrations level out and become as close as possible to the vibrations of the physical plane of planet Earth.

In that case, we dive under the dense veil, and our consciousness can no longer comprehend the higher understanding.

It is very rare that a partial incarnation of an Ascended Master arrives into conditions on planet Earth in which she can remember her Divinity and withstand the trials of life.

That is exactly why we use the institution of Messengers. A person who had taken on the duties of being our Messenger before incarnation, just like any one of you who is willing to Serve the Brotherhood, undergoes the trials and tests during the period of at least seven years. After that, she takes on certain responsibilities in the form of a vow. Then we take her through another round of tests, but those tests are more advanced. And when the individual stands the tests for the position of Messenger, we give her the opportunity to Serve. This opportunity is supported with the so-called "mantles of the Messenger." In other words, we use a certain amount of energy in order to constantly maintain the energy potential of the Messenger at a certain level.

It is thanks to the mantles that the Messenger is able to maintain proper orienting points in the conditions of your world. And those of you who sincerely accept our Messenger and are ready to Serve her and in this person the Brotherhood, automatically connect to our protective field.

Yet, as soon as low-quality thoughts and, most importantly, thoughts of criticism against our Messenger come to your mind or you perform an action or say any words against our Messenger, the protection loses its effect, and all the energy that until this moment has sustained your consciousness through our Messenger, turns into karma.

It is very wise to maintain proper attitude toward our Messenger not as a perfect manifestation but as a person who has been trusted to represent the interests of the Brotherhood in the physical plane.

Like everything in your world, the mantle of the Messenger has a dual effect. On the one hand, it helps to maintain the consciousness of people who are sincerely devoted to the Messenger and feel love and respect toward her, at a relatively high level. On the other hand, any action, thought, or feeling of criticism toward our

Messenger turns against the person who opposes our Messenger and creates a very serious karma that is equal to karma with God.

Today my talk has provided certain explanations for you regarding the possibility of incarnation of the Masters and the institution of Messengers, with the help of which the Masters complete many tasks in your world.

I think that for many of you, my talk today is useful and insightful.

I AM Jesus.

I wish to help each one of you

June 24, 2012

I AM Jesus.

I have come to you now, today, because I have something to tell you. Thanks to Divine mercy, other Masters and I can still come and give our Teaching to humankind of Earth. My duty is to tell you about the Path that I was following and that each of you can follow. This is the Path of Love, the Path that is lying within your hearts. Only at the level of your heart do all the contradictions and everything that separates you disappear. Then, when the majority of humanity raises their vibrations to the level where they approach the vibrations of the heart chakra, only at this level of consciousness will all the negative manifestations and everything around you that does not conform to the Divine standard disappear.

Therefore, each of you who wish to get closer to God can exert an effort and desire to follow my Path, the Path that I teach.

Many people want to heal and even more people wish to perform miracles, to walk on water, and to revive the dead. But I taught much more important things that escape your consciousness because they do not lie in the field of outer manifestations but in the field of the hidden qualities of your soul.

In the folds of your soul, you should find your Divine opportunity, your Path to the eternal world, your Path to peace and goodness, and to meekness and humility.

It is exactly the qualities of your soul that determine your further evolution. And this has nothing to do with the outer manifestation.

The Inner Path, the Divine Path, is always with you all the way through your incarnation. However, very few people recognize this Path and follow it.

There are too many temptations in your world. And modern ways of communication and mass media are so trumpet-tongued that you cannot hear the voice of your heart behind the noise and commotion.

I can only be present in your hearts. Then, when you are able to hear the voice of your heart, you will also be able to recognize me. You become able to see me and communicate with me.

We are separated by the illusion that is remaining around you. But the commotion of the world is fading and vanishing thanks to the efforts of those who aspire, those who are devoted to God, who believe and love.

Therefore, I have come today in order to talk to you about your aspiration. The quality of your aspiration and persistence is able to overcome any barriers that stand between you and me.

Just wish to apply effort; just wish to follow my Path. I promise my support to each of you. And the power of my support and help depends on the strength of your aspiration.

I wish to help each one of you. And I understand your difficulties very well. In its last convulsions, the illusion tries to keep you from your return to God. And this becomes more and more obvious. The most barbaric arsenal of means is deployed in order to alienate you from God and from my Path: blaring music, alcohol and drugs, fascination with objects, and escalating desires to possess things. All this is an extreme manifestation of the opposing forces. And then, when you are able to rise in your consciousness above your attachments and desires, your four lower bodies become disenchanted with the lure of the illusion and you will become able to see me and perceive the Divine world.

Your return to my world only depends on your own aspiration and your inner choice. You do not need to call anyone to come with you. You do not need to vociferously demand that people come to God.

I will reveal a secret to you. And the mystery of this secret is that each of you is able to pull millions of souls out of the debris of the illusion by showing them the Path, by becoming the Path itself. But for this you do not need to call anybody or force anyone to follow the Path with you. The Divine world acts with finesse. And the harmony that you obtain within yourself will do the work for you. Your vibrations, your state of consciousness itself will show the Path to those souls who are ready to return Home.

Your illusion is dense only while you believe in it and are attached to it in your consciousness. As soon as you reveal another reality within your being, the illusion of your world fades and disappears like a night fog. The twilight of your consciousness is illuminated by the Divine Light emanating from your hearts.

The Divine world is not somewhere far away from the world. The Divine world is constantly near you. And whether you will be able to cross the threshold between our worlds and approach me depends only on your everyday efforts.

I am where you are. I am standing right in front of you and extending my helping hand to you. See me. Disperse the fog of illusion that is blinding your eyes, and take my hand.

You are able to overcome all the barriers on your Path. As soon as you manage to believe in God and accept His help, you will feel relieved. And the most difficult life situations that you face will not dishearten you anymore, because you will obtain the understanding that you will pass through all the difficulties. No matter how hard the Path is, you will be led by Hope, Faith, and Love.

All the obstacles can be overcome when are walking with God.

The inner Light will illuminate the Path for you in the worst life situations.

I believe in you and in your aspiration and devotion. Together we can overcome any resistance and reach the part of the Path from where a breathtaking view of the Divine summit opens up.

I AM Jesus.

On the foundations of the Teaching and the continuity of the transmission of the Teaching

June 27, 2013

I AM Jesus.

The followers of the Teaching, who followed in my footsteps after my crucifixion and ascension, called me the Son of God.

Many points of the Teaching that I was sharing with my disciples during my life underwent many changes over the course of time; at times they were slightly distorted and at times they underwent fundamental changes and even acquired an opposite meaning. It is not so much the fault of my disciples because of the ignorance that was prevailing on Earth at that time and, unfortunately, it continues to prevail in your time.

It took 2000 years for the people of Earth who called themselves Christians, at least for some part of them, to start perceiving my Teaching on reincarnation and my Teaching on the Law of Karma.

Even if you impartially reread the texts of the Gospel that you have now, then you will find that hints about these fundamental Teachings are scattered here and there. And this is obvious to everyone who reads the text not just through their external consciousness but also with all their hearts.

Many points being lost or not given sufficient significance could lead to the incorrect interpretation of the Teaching and of its essence.

The words about the man liable to decay and the imperishable man cannot be understood if you do not know about the Law of Karma and the Law of Reincarnation. In the same way, these words cannot be understood if you consider man as flesh and blood without taking into account his soul and the Spirit of God that resides in each person.

It is possible to appeal to the human conscience and to threaten it with Divine punishment, and this can have an influence on an undeveloped consciousness. But when the person with a curious mind starts learning the laws of the universe, the intimidation and calls to order do not work anymore. In this case, the worst thing that could happen would be if a person turns away from God and His servants and rejects the church and the faith itself.

However, more developed individuals can go further in their cognition of the world and its organization. The words of the Gospel — "whatever one sows, that will he also reap" — start to acquire a genuine meaning for them.

Indeed, it is impossible to explain to the external consciousness why one must follow the moral law and why one should follow certain moral norms and regulations without understanding the connection between the deeds of a person in this incarnation and in the previous one, and their consequences.

Each individual must come to realize the connection between their actions and the consequences of those actions. Without understanding this connection, it is impossible to explain many things in your world that seem unfair, such as property inequalities, caste privileges for some people and poverty for others, incurable diseases burdening some people and excellent health for others.

Why do some people die prematurely while others live a long life? The reasons for all of this can only be found in the previous lives, and at times this is completely impossible to explain in terms of the current incarnation and the circumstances of one life.

Therefore, one of the tasks that the Ascended Masters strive for is the transmission of the Teaching in a form that can be perceived by the consciousness of the current generation. The continuity of the transmission of the Teaching is the guarantee that humankind will constantly have a lifeline at their disposal that can pull those who strive to follow the Path out of the rough waters of life.

Without the lifeline of the Teaching, without its continuous updating and continuous transmission, humankind will slide into the way of life of an animal and will not be able to distinguish between the Light and the darkness, the truth and the lie, the virtuous behavior and the sinful one.

Unfortunately, despite all our efforts that we tirelessly apply, some part of humankind does not pay attention to our instructions and continues to live as if only death is ahead.

The generations of people who walk away from God in their consciousness, who do not aspire to know the Eternal Law of the Universe, create the consequences for their descendants that lead to complete degradation and immorality. And the breach of all moral norms has already become the norm.

If the knowledge of the Law of Karma is obliterated in the consciousness of generations of people, then each successive generation falls deeper and deeper into godlessness and violation of the moral law because people cease to feel the connection between the troubles that fall to them and their own deeds that lead to these troubles.

The institution of the church, designed to keep people within the Divine Law, becomes less important as people lose their faith and walk away from the moral ideals.

In these conditions the only salvation for humankind is to return to God and the true faith as a state of consciousness. The perception of God, not as an old man who is represented in the icons of a church but as the inner Light running through all of Creation and residing in all the beings on the altar of their hearts, can provide assistance to humanity at this stage of development.

The concept of God, who does not live in temples but fills the whole ambient space by Himself, can be understood by the minds of people at this stage of evolutionary development. And in the chaos that exists in the world now, the only regulator and guarantor of stability is the inner governor, the human conscience, or God, who resides in every human being.

We come to you in the hope that many of you can understand the truths being given by us at this stage of human development. We sincerely hope that these truths will germinate in your hearts and you will become one with the Teaching that we are giving.

When you reach this stage of your development, you become one with the inner truth of God residing in your hearts, and you become a source of Light and knowledge for your world. And the more light-bearers that reside in the world, the stronger the guarantee is that the world will restore its stability and stop and shake off all incorrect teachings and faiths that take advantage of people's ignorance and fears in the mercenary interests of certain individuals.

I do hope that each of you who read our Messages given through our Messenger will acquire an inexhaustible source of inner faith and resistance to any external imperfect manifestations of the world, thanks to this adamant faith.

I AM Jesus.

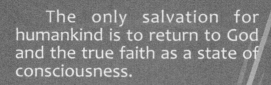

The only salvation for humankind is to return to God and the true faith as a state of consciousness.

Beloved Jesus,
June 27, 2013

BOOKS BY
TATYANA N. MICKUSHINA
MASTERS OF WISDOM SERIES

Each of the Masters of Wisdom strives to give us what they consider most vital at the present moment of transition. Every message contains the energies of different Masters who give those messages. The Masters speak about the current historical moment on planet Earth. They tell us about energy and vibrations, about the illusion of this world and about the Divine Reality, about the Higher Self of a human and about his lower bodies. They give us concrete recommendations on exactly how to change our own consciousness and continue on the evolutionary Path. It is recommended that you prepare yourself for reading every message very carefully. You have to tune to the Master who is giving the message with the help of proper music, with the help of the Master's image, or by using a prayer or a meditation before reading the Message. That way you align your energies, elevate your consciousness, and the messages can benefit you.

SAINT GERMAIN

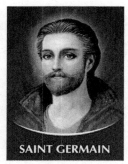

SAINT GERMAIN

Saint Germain is at present an Ascended Master, the Hierarch of the New Age. In his last incarnation as the Count de Saint Germain in the 18th century, he exerted a great influence on the course of world history. The Messages of Master Saint Germain are charged with optimism and faith in the forthcoming Golden Age! He teaches about preparing for a New Age by transforming our consciousness, and reminds us: "Joy and Love come to you when your Faith is steadfast, when you rely in your consciousness on God and the Ascended Hosts."

SANAT KUMARA

SANAT KUMARA

Masters of Wisdom, first of all Sanat Kumara, remind us about our Divine origin and call us to wake up to a Higher reality, because Divine Reality by its love, wisdom, and beauty exceeds any of the most wonderful aspects of our physical world. The Messages of Sanat Kumara include Teachings on true and false messengers, Communities of the Holy Spirit, responsibility for the duties that one has taken upon him/herself before their incarnation, the right use of the money energy, the choice of everyone between the Eternal and the perishable world, overcoming the ego, the Path of Initiations, and many other topics.

MORYA

Messages from the Teacher, Master Morya, have been given through Helena Blavatsky in the 19th century, Helena and Nicholas Roerich in the period around 1920-1950, and Mark and Elizabeth Clare Prophet in the 1960's. Master Morya is still actively working on the Spiritual plane to help the humanity of the World. Now the Masters continue their work through a Messenger from Russia, Tatyana Mickushina.

This book contains selected Messages from Master Morya. Many Teachings are given in the

Messages, including the Teachings about the correct actions on the physical plane, Service to Brotherhood, the attainment of the qualities of a disciple such as devotion, persistence, aspiration, and discipline. Some aspects of the Teaching about changing of consciousness are also introduced here.

SHIVA

SHIVA

The present volume contains selected Messages of Lord Shva. Many Teachings are given in these Messages; including the Teaching about God, the Teaching about Discernment of reality from illusion: which helps to ascend to a new level of consciousness and also new aspects of the Guru-chela relationship are considered.

Author page of T. N. Mickushina on Amazon:

amazon.com/author/tatyana_mickushina

OTHERS BOOKS BY TATYANA N. MICKUSHINA

About Yoga and Meditation

A Lecture at a Session of the University of Life Ethics by T. N. Mickushina March 27, 2015 (Materials to the seminars) .

This book is based on the audio recorded lecture by Tatyana N. Mickushina at the University of Life Ethics on March 27, 2015. This lecture explains why so few people can master the practice of true meditation and what those who cannot engage in meditation practice can do.

Treasures of Divine Wisdom

The multivolume book, Words of Wisdom by Tatyana Mickushina, has several thousand pages of text. This book was created to meet the spiritual needs of busy people who are unable to spend much time reading. The book includes the most concise and significant quotations from the book Words of Wisdom.

Masters of Wisdom

JESUS

**Dictations received by the Messenger
Tatyana Nicholaevna Mickushina
from 2005 through 2013**

Please, leave your review about this book at
amazon.com. This will greatly help in spreading the
Teaching of the Ascended Masters given through the
Messenger Tatyana Mickushina.

Websites:

http://sirius-eng.net (English version)
http://sirius-ru.net (Russian version)

Books by T.N.Mickushina on amazon.com:
amazon.com/author/tatyana_mickushina

Cover artwork by Munir Alawi
www.muniralawi.info

Made in the USA
Columbia, SC
13 April 2022

58893801R00083